. . .

W A L T   W H I T M A N

THE WALT WHITMAN READER

SELECTIONS FROM *LEAVES OF GRASS*

COURAGE
BOOKS

an imprint of
RUNNING PRESS
Philadelphia, Pennsylvania

The text of this volume is excerpted from the 1891–92 edition of
Leaves of Grass published by David McKay, Philadelphia, in 1900 and made
available through the courtesy of the Miriam Coffin Canaday Library,
Bryn Mawr College.

The essay "Observations on Walt Whitman" by T.S. Eliot was first published
in *The Nation & The Athenaeum*, XL (Dec. 18, 1926). Reprinted with
permission of Mrs. Valerie Eliot and Faber and Faber, Ltd.
Copyright © 1926 by Mrs. Valerie Eliot.

The essay "Whitman" by D.H. Lawrence from *Studies in Classic American
Literature*. Copyright © 1923 by Thomas Seltzer, Inc., renewed 1950 by
Frieda Lawrence. Copyright © 1961 by The Estate of the late
Mrs. Frieda Lawrence. Reprinted with permission of Viking Penguin,
a division of Penguin Books USA Inc.

Canadian representatives: General Publishing Co., Ltd.,
30 Lesmill Road, Don Mills, Ontario M3B 2T6.

International representatives: Worldwide Media Services, Inc.,
30 Montgomery Street, Jersey City, New Jersey 07302.

9 8 7 6 5 4 3 2 1
Digit on the right indicates the number of this printing.

Library of Congress Cataloging-in-publication Number 92–54931

ISBN 1–56138–268–X

Cover illustration by Lars Hokanson
Portrait of Walt Whitman provided by The Granger Collection, New York
Cover design by Toby Schmidt
Interior design by Elizabeth Schwartz
Typography: ITC Berkeley Oldstyle, by Deborah Lugar

Published by Courage Books, an imprint of
Running Press Book Publishers
125 South Twenty-second Street
Philadelphia, Pennsylvania 19103

. . .

INTRODUCTION

WALT WHITMAN, CONSIDERED by some of his literary con-
temporaries – including Ralph Waldo Emerson and D.H.
Lawrence – to be the "greatest American poet," personified the
vitality and diversity of mid-nineteenth-century America.

Born in 1819 on Long Island, New York, he spent his
childhood alternating between the bucolic countryside of Long
Island and the hustle and bustle of Brooklyn's mercantile
district. By late childhood, Whitman had left school and
established his financial independence, working as a typesetter
and newspaperman. Although he ended his formal education
early, he enriched his worldly education by immersing himself
in the life of the city. By the time he was 28 years old, he
became the editor of the *Brooklyn Eagle*, and as he explored
the vast cultural resources and the workaday life of New York,
his newspaper articles addressed themes ranging form
abolition to bank reform.

An essential aspect of Whitman's nature was his roving
spirit; after just a few years, he left the newspaper, traveling to
New Orleans and back to Brooklyn. His outspoken, liberal
views created neither a popular following nor career stability,
and during the next decade he had stints at journalism,
teaching, and pamphleteering. During these years Whitman's
political and philosophical sensibilities began to coalesce, and
in 1855 he published the first edition of *Leaves of Grass*, a
collection of twelve poems.

The leading intellect of the time, Ralph Waldo Emerson,
praised Whitman's poems, writing, "I greet you at the begin-
ning of a great career." Whitman was surely influenced by this

great American thinker; many of his poetic themes expanded upon Emerson's new and revolutionary philosophy of the freedom of the spirit, the universality of human experience, and the diversity of the uniquely American way of life.

Whitman published several subsequent editions of *Leaves of Grass*, each time enlarging the collection of poems to embrance the varying experiences of the nation and its individuals. He celebrated the communion of souls in *I Sing the Body Electric*, the worthiness of a hard day's work in *Crossing Brooklyn Ferry*, and despaired of the destructiveness of war in *When Lilacs Last in the Dooryard Bloom'd*.

Walt Whitman spent his later years in Camden, New Jersey, and the house on Mickle Street where he died in 1892 is now a national historic site. The year before his death, he authorized a Philadelphia publisher, David McKay, to print the ninth, "deathbed" edition of *Leaves of Grass*, and it is that edition from which we gather a selection of Whitman's best-loved poems.

. . .

CONTENTS

INTRODUCTION

One's-Self I Sing 9
As I Ponder'd In Silence 9
In Cabin'd Ships at Sea 10
To Thee, Old Cause! 12
Starting from Paumanok 12
Walt Whitman (Song of Myself) 29
From Pent-up Aching Rivers 105
I Sing the Body Electric 108
In Paths Untrodden 119
Recorders Ages Hence 120
Salut au Monde 121
American Feuillage 135
Song of the Broad-Axe 143
Song of the Open Road 157
As I Lay with Head in Your Lap, Camerado 171
Crossing Brooklyn Ferry 172
Now List to my Morning's Romanza 181
I Hear America Singing 185
Carol of Occupations 186
The Sleepers 197
Carol of Words 210
There was a Child went Forth 218
Drum-Taps 221
As I Sat Alone by Blue Ontario's Shores 224
Mannahatta 244
Passage to India 246

Proud Music of The Storm 258
When Lilacs Last in the Door-yard Bloom'd 266
O Captain! My Captain! 278
A Noiseless Patient Spider. 279
Out of the Cradle Endlessly Rocking 280
A Carol of Harvest for 1867 288
Sparkles from The Wheel 296
As a Strong Bird on Pinions Free 297

ESSAYS 307

ONE'S-SELF I SING

First published in 1870

ONE'S-SELF I sing—a simple, separate Person;
Yet utter the word Democratic, the word *En-masse*.

Of Physiology from top to toe I sing;
Not physiognomy alone, nor brain alone, is worthy for the
          muse—I say the Form complete is worthier far;
The Female equally with the male I sing.

Of Life immense in passion, pulse, and power,
Cheerful—for freest action form'd, under the laws divine,
The Modern Man I sing.

AS I PONDER'D IN SILENCE

First published in 1870

1

AS I PONDER'D in silence,
Returning upon my poems, considering, lingering long,
A Phantom arose before me, with distrustful aspect,
Terrible in beauty, age, and power,
The genius of poets of old lands,
As to me directing like flame its eyes,
With finger pointing to many immortal songs,
And menacing voice, *What singest thou?* it said;
Know'st thou not, there is but one theme for ever-enduring bards?

And that is the theme of War, the fortune of battles,
The making of perfect soldiers?

2

Be it so, then I answer'd,
I too, haughty Shade, also sing war—and a longer and greater one
than any,
Waged in my book with varying fortune—with flight, advance, and
retreat—Victory deferr'd and wavering,
(Yet, methinks, certain, or as good as certain, at the last,)—The
field the world;
For life and death—for the Body, and for the eternal Soul,
Lo! I too am come, chanting the chant of battles,
I, above all, promote brave soldiers.

IN CABIN'D SHIPS AT SEA

First published in 1870

1

IN CABIN'D SHIPS, at sea,
The boundless blue on every side expanding,
With whistling winds and music of the waves—the large
imperious waves—In such,
Or some lone bark, buoy'd on the dense marine,
Where, joyous, full of faith, spreading white sails,
She cleaves the ether, mid the sparkle and the foam of day, or
under many a star at night,
By sailors young and old, haply will I, a reminiscence of the
land, be read,
In full rapport at last.

2

Here are our thoughts—voyagers' thoughts,
Here not the land, firm land, alone appears, may then by them
        be said;
The sky o'erarches here—we fell the undulating deck beneath
        our feet,
We feel the long pulsation—ebb and flow of endless motion;
The tones of unseen mystery—the vague and vast suggestions of the
        briny world—the liquid-flowing syllables,
The perfume, the faint creaking of the cordage, the melancholy
        rhythm,
The boundless vista, and the horizon far and dim, are all here,
And this is Ocean's poem.

3

Then falter not, O book! fulfil your destiny!
You, not a reminiscence of the land alone,
You too, as a lone bark, cleaving the ether—purpos'd I know
        not whither—yet ever full of faith,
Consort to every ship that sails—sail you!
Bear forth to them, folded, my love—(Dear mariners! for you I
        fold it here, in every leaf;)
Speed on, my Book! spread your white sails, my little bark,
        athwart the imperious waves!
Chant on—sail on—bear o'er the boundless blue, from me, to
        every shore,
This song for mariners and all their ships.

To Thee, Old Cause!

First published in 1870

To thee, old Cause!
Thou peerless, passionate, good cause!
Thou stern, remorseless, sweet Idea!
Deathless throughout the ages, races, lands!
After a strange, sad war – great war for thee,
(I think all war through time was really fought, and ever will
          be really fought, for thee;)
These chants for thee – the eternal march of thee.

Thou orb of many orbs!
Thou seething principle! Thou well-kept, latent germ!
          Thou centre!
Around the idea of thee the strange sad war revolving,
With all its angry and vehement play of causes,
(With yet unknown results to come, for thrice a thousand years,)
These recitatives for thee – my Book and the War are one,
Merged in its spirit I and mine – as the contest hinged on thee,
As a wheel on its axis turns, this Book, unwitting to itself,
Around the Idea of thee.

Starting from Paumanok

First published in 1860 under title of "Proto-Leaf"

1

Starting from fish-shape Paumanok, where I was born,
Well-begotten, and rais'd by a perfect mother;

After roaming many lands—lover of populous pavements;
Dweller in Mannahatta, my city—or on southern savannas;
Or a soldier camp'd, or carrying my knapsack and gun—or a
        miner in California;
Or rude in my home in Dakota's woods, my diet meat, my
        drink from the spring;
Or withdrawn to use and meditate in some deep recess,
Far from the clank of crowds, intervals passing, rapt
        and happy;
Aware of the fresh free giver, the flowing Missouri—aware of
        mighty Niagara;
Aware of the buffalo herds, grazing the plains—the hirsute and
        strong-breasted bull;
Of earth, rocks, Fifth-month flowers, experienced—stars, rain,
        snow, my amaze;
Having studied the mocking-bird's tones, and the
        mountain-hawk's,
And heard at dusk the unrival'd one, the hermit thrush from
        the swamp-cedars,
Solitary, singing in the West, I strike up for a New World.

2

Victory, union, faith, identity, time,
The indissoluble compacts, riches, mystery,
Eternal progress, the kosmos, the modern reports.

This, then, is life;
Here is what has come to the surface after so many throes
        and convulsions.
How curious! How real!
Underfoot the divine soil—overhead the sun.

See, revolving, the globe;
The ancestor-continents, away, group'd together;
The present and future continents, north and south, with the
      isthmus between.

See, vast, trackless spaces;
As in a dream, they change, they swiftly fill;
Countless masses debouch upon them;
They are now cover'd with the foremost people, arts,
      institutions, known.

See, projected, through time,
For me, an audience interminable.

With firm and regular step they wend – they never stop,
Successions of men, Americanos, a hundred millions;
One generation playing its part, and passing on;
Another generation playing its part, and passing on in its turn,
With faces turn'd sideways or backward towards me, to listen,
With eyes retrospective towards me,

3

Americanos! conquerors! marches humanitarian;
Foremost! century marches! Libertad! masses!
For you a programme of chants.

Chants of the prairies;
Chants of the long-running Mississippi, and down to the
      Mexican sea;
Chants of Ohio, Indiana, Illinois, Iowa, Wisconsin
      and Minnesota;

Chants going forth from the centre, from Kansas, and thence,
      equi-distant,
Shooting in pulses of fire, ceaseless, to vivify all.

4

In the Year 80 of The States,
My tongue, every atom of my blood, form'd from this soil,
      this air,
Born here of parents born here, from parents the same, and
      their parents the same,
I, now thirty-six years old, in perfect health, begin,
Hoping to cease not till death.

Creeds and schools in abeyance,
(Retiring back a while, sufficed at what they are, but never
      forgotten,)
I harbor, for good or bad—I permit to speak, at every hazard,
Nature now without check, with original energy.

5

Take my leaves, America! take them, South, and take
      them, North!
Make welcome for them everywhere, for they are your
      own offspring;
Surround them, East and West! for they would surround you;
And you precedents! connect lovingly with them, for they
      connect lovingly with you.

I conn'd old times;
I sat studying at the feet of the great masters:
Now, if eligible, O that the great masters might return and
      study me!

In the name of These States, shall I scorn the antique?
Why These are the children of the antique, to justify it.

6

Dead poets, philosophs, priests,
Martyrs, artists, inventors, governments long since,
Language-shapers, on other shores,
Nations once powerful, now reduced, withdrawn, or desolate,
I dare not proceed till I respectfully credit what you have left,
        wafted hither:
I have perused it – own it is admirable, (moving awhile
        among it;)
Think nothing can ever be greater – nothing can ever deserve
        more than it deserves;
Regarding it all intently a long while – then dismissing it,
I stand in my place, with my own day, here.

Here lands female and male;
Here the heir-ship and heiress-ship of the world – here the
        flame of materials;
Here Spirituality, the translatress, the openly-avow'd,
The ever-tending, the finale of visible forms;
The satisfier, after due long-waiting, now advancing,
Yes, here comes my mistress, the Soul.

7

The SOUL:
Forever and forever – longer than soil is brown and solid –
        longer than water ebbs and flows.

I will make the poems of materials, for I think they are to be
        the most spiritual poems;
And I will make the poems of my body and of mortality,
For I think I shall then supply myself with the poems of my
        Soul, and of immortality.

I will make a song for These States, that no one State may
        under any circumstances be subjected to another State;
And I will make a song that there shall be comity by day and
        by night between all The States, and between any two
        of them:
And I will make a song for the ears of the President, full of
        weapons with menacing points,
And behind the weapons countless dissatisfied faces:
−And a song make I, of the One form'd out of all;
The fang'd and glittering One whose head is over all;
Resolute, warlike One, including and over all;
(However high the head of any else, that head is over all.)

I will acknowledge contemporary lands;
I will trail the whole geography of the globe, and salute
        courteously every city large and small;
And employments! I will put in my poems, that with you is
        heroism, upon land and sea;
And I will report all heroism from an American point of view.

I will sing the song of companionship;
I will show what alone must finally compact These;
I believe These are to found their own ideal of manly love,
        indicating it in me;
I will therefore let flame from me the burning fires that were
        threatening to consume me;

I will lift what has too long kept down those smouldering fires;
I will give them complete abandonment;
I will write the evangel-poem of comrades, and of love;
(For who but I should understand love, with all its sorrow and
       joy?
And who but I should be the poet of comrades?)

8

I am the credulous man of qualities, ages, races;
I advance from the people in their own spirit;
Here is what sings unrestricted faith.

Omnes! Omnes! let others ignore what they may;
I make the poem of evil also—I commemorate that part also;
I am myself just as much evil as good, and my nation is—And I
      say there is in fact no evil;
(Or if there is, I say it is just as important to you, to the land,
      or to me, as anything else.)
I too, following many, and follow'd by many, inaugurate a
      Religion—I descend into the arena;
(It may be I am destin'd to utter the loudest cries there, the
      winner's pealing shouts;
Who knows? they may rise from me yet, and soar above
      every thing.)

Each is not for its own sake;
I say the whole earth, and all the stars in the sky, are for
      Religion's sake.

I say no man has ever yet been half devout enough;
None has ever yet adored or worship'd half enough;
None has begun to think how divine he himself is, and how
       certain the future is.

I say that the real and permanent grandeur of These States
       must be their Religion;
Otherwise there is no real and permanent grandeur:
(Nor character, nor life worthy the name, without Religion;
Nor land, nor man or woman, without Religion.)

9

What are you doing, young man?
Are you so earnest—so given up to literature, science,
       art, amours?
These ostensible realities, politics, points?
Your ambition or business, whatever it may be?

It is well—Against such I say not a word—I am their poet also;
But behold! such swiftly subside—burnt up for Religion's sake;
For not all matter is fuel to heat, impalpable flame, the
       essential life of the earth,
Any more than such are to Religion.

10

What do you seek, so pensive and silent?
What do you need, Camerado?
Dear son! do you think it is love?

Listen, dear son—listen, America, daughter or son!
It is a painful thing to love a man or woman to excess—and yet
       it satisfies—it is great;

But there is something else very great—it makes the
      whole coincide;
It, magnificent, beyond materials, with continuous hands,
      sweeps and provides for all.

11

Know you! solely to drop in the earth the germs of a
      greater Religion,
The following chants, each for its kind, I sing.

My comrade!
For you, to share with me, two greatnesses—and a third one,
      rising inclusive and more resplendent,
The greatness of Love and Democracy—and the greatness
      of Religion.

Melange mine own! the unseen and the seen;
Mysterious ocean where the streams empty;
Prophetic spirit of materials shifting and flickering around me;
Living beings, identities, now doubtless near us, in the air, that
      we know not of;
Contact daily and hourly that will not release me;
These selecting—these, in hints, demanded of me.

Not he, with a daily kiss, onward from childhood kissing me,
Has winded and twisted around me that which holds me
      to him,
Any more than I am held to the heavens, to the spiritual world,
And to the identities of the Gods, my lovers, faithful and true,
After what they have done to me, suggesting themes.

O such themes! Equalities!
O amazement of things! O divine average!
O warblings under the sun—usher'd, as now, or at noon,
      or setting!
O strain, musical, flowing through ages—now reaching hither!
I take to your reckless and composite chords—I add to them,
      and cheerfully pass them forward.

12

As I have walk'd in Alabama my morning walk,
I have seen where the she-bird, the mocking-bird, sat on her
      nest in the briers, hatching her brood.

I have seen the he-bird also;
I have paused to hear him, near at hand, inflating his throat,
      and joyfully singing.

And while I paused, it came to me that what he really sang for
      was not there only,
Nor for his mate, nor himself only, nor all sent back by
      the echoes;
But subtle, clandestine, away beyond,
A charge transmitted, and gift occult, for those being born.

13

Democracy!
Near at hand to you a throat is now inflating itself and
      joyfully singing.

Ma femme!
For the brood beyond us and of us,
For those who belong here, and those to come,

I, exultant, to be ready for them, will now shake out carols
        stronger and haughtier than have ever yet been heard
        upon earth.
I will make the songs of passion, to give them their way,
And your songs, outlaw'd offenders—for I scan you with
        kindred eyes, and carry you with me the same as any.

I will make the true poem of riches,
To earn for the body and the mind whatever adheres, and goes
        forward, and is not dropt by death.

I will effuse egotism, and show it underlying all—and I will be
        the bard of personality;
And I will show of male and female that either is but the equal
        of the other;
And sexual organs and acts! do you concentrate in me—for I
        am determin'd to tell you with courageous clear voice,
        to prove you illustrious;
And I will show that there is no imperfection in the present—
        and can be none in the future;
And I will show that whatever happens to anybody, it may be
        turn'd to beautiful results—and I will show that nothing
        can happen more beautiful than death;
And I will thread a thread through my poems that time and
        events are compact,
And that all the things of the universe are perfect miracles,
        each as profound as any.

I will not make poems with reference to parts;
But I will make leaves, poems, poemets, songs, says, thoughts,
        with reference to ensemble:
And I will not sing with reference to a day, but with reference
        to all days;

And I will not make a poem, nor the least part of a poem, but
      has reference to the Soul;
(Because, having look'd at the objects of the universe, I find
      there is no one, nor any particle of one, but has
      reference to the Soul.)

14

Was somebody asking to see the Soul?
See! your own shape and countenance—persons, substances,
      beasts, the trees, the running rivers, the rocks
      and sands.

All hold spiritual joys, and afterwards loosen them:
How can the real body ever die, and be buried?

Of your real body, and any man's or woman's real body,
Item for item, it will elude the hands of the corpse-cleaners,
      and pass to fitting spheres,
Carrying what has accrued to it from the moment of birth to
      the moment of death.

Not the types set up by the printer return their impression, the
      meaning, the main concern,
Any more than a man's substance and life, or a woman's
      substance and life, return in the body and the Soul,
Indifferently before death and after death.

Behold! the body includes and is the meaning, the main
      concern—and includes and is the Soul;
Whoever you are! how superb and how divine is your body, or
      any part of it.

15

Whoever you are! to you endless announcements.

Daughter of the lands, did you wait for your poet?
Did you wait for one with a flowing mouth and indicative
    hand?

Toward the male of The States, and toward the female of
    The States,
Live words—words to the lands.

O the lands! interlink'd, food-yielding lands!
Land of coal and iron! Land of gold! Lands of cotton,
    sugar, rice!
Land of wheat, beef, pork! Land of wool and hemp! Land of
    the apple and grape!
Land of the pastoral plains, the grass-fields of the world! Land
    of those sweet-air'd interminable plateaus!
Land of the herd, the garden, the healthy house of adobie!
Lands where the northwest Columbia winds, and where the
    southwest Colorado winds!
Land of the eastern Chesapeake! Land of the Delaware!
Land of Ontario, Erie, Huron, Michigan!
Land of the Old Thirteen! Massachusetts land! Land of
    Vermont and Connecticut!
Land of the ocean shores! Land of sierras and peaks!
Land of boatmen and sailors! Fishermen's land!
Inextricable lands! the clutch'd together! the passionate ones!
The side by side! the elder and younger brothers! the
    bony-limb'd!

The great women's land! the feminine! the experienced sisters
        and the inexperienced sisters!
Far breath'd land! Arctic braced! Mexican breez'd! the diverse!
        the compact!
The Pennsylvanian! the Virginian! the double Carolinian!
O all and each well-loved by me! my intrepid nations! O I at
        any rate include you all with perfect love!
I cannot be discharged from you! not from one, any sooner
        than another!
O Death! O for all that, I am yet of you, unseen, this hour,
        with irrepressible love,
Walking New England, a friend, a traveler,
Splashing my bare feet in the edge of the summer ripples, on
        Paumanok's sands,
Crossing the prairies – dwelling again in Chicago – dwelling in
        every town,
Observing shows, births, improvements, structures, arts,
Listening to the orators and the oratresses in public halls,
Of and throughout The States, as during life – each man and
        woman my neighbor,
The Louisianian, the Georgian, as near to me, and I as near to
        him and her,
The mississippian and Arkansian yet with me – and I yet with
        any of them;
Yet upon the plains west of the spinal river – yet in my house
        of adobie,
Yet returning eastward – yet in the Sea-Side State, or in Maryland,
Yet Kanadian, cheerily braving the winter – the snow and ice
        welcome to me,
Yet a true son either of Maine, or of the Granite State, or of the
        Narragansett Bay State, or of the Empire State;

Yet sailing to other shores to annex the same—yet welcoming
    every new brother;
Hereby applying these leaves to the new ones, from the hour
    they unite with the old ones;
Coming among the new ones myself, to be their companion
    and equal—coming personally to you now;
Enjoining you to acts, characters, spectacles, with me.

16

With me, with firm holding—yet haste, haste on.

For your life, adhere to me!
Of all the men of the earth, I only can unloose you and
    toughen you;
I may have to be persuaded many times before I consent to
    give myself really to you—but what of that?
Must not Nature be persuaded many times?

No dainty dolce affettuoso I;
Bearded, sun-burnt, gray-neck'd, forbidding, I have arrived,
To be wrestled with as I pass, for the solid prizes of the
    universe;
For such I afford whoever can persevere to win them.

17

On my way a moment I pause;
Here for you! and here for America!
Still the Present I raise aloft—Still the Future of The States I
    harbinge, glad and sublime;
And for the Past, I pronounce what the air holds of the
    red aborigines.

The red aboriginies!
Leaving natural breaths, sounds of rain and winds, calls as of
        birds and animals in the woods, syllabled to us
        for names;
Okonee, Koosa, Ottawa, Monongahela, Sauk, Natchez,
        Chattahoochee, Kaqueta, Oronoco,
Wabash, Miami, Saginaw, Chippewa, Oshkosh, Walla-Walla;
Leaving such to The States, they melt, they depart, charging the
        water and the land with names.

18

O expanding and swift! O henceforth,
Elements, breeds, adjustments, turbulent, quick, and audacious;
A world primal again—Vistas of glory, incessant and branching;
A new race, dominating previous ones, and grander far—with
        new contests,
New politics, new literatures and religions, new inventions
        and arts.

These! my voice announcing—I will sleep no more, but arise;
You oceans that have been calm within me! how I feel you,
        fathomless, stirring, preparing unprecedented waves
        and storms.

19

See! steamers steaming through my poems!
See, in my poems immigrants continually coming and landing;
See, in arriere, the wigwam, the trail, the hunter's hut, the
        flatboat, the maize-leaf, the claim, the rude fence, and
        the backwoods village;

See, on the one side the Western Sea, and on the other the
      Eastern Sea, how they advance and retreat upon my
      poems, as upon their own shores.

See, pastures and forests in my poems – See, animals, wild and
      tame – See, beyond the Kanzas, countless herds of
      buffalo, feeding on short curly grass;
See, in my poems, cities, solid, vast, inland, with paved streets,
      with iron and stone edifices, ceaseless vehicles,
      and commerce;
See, the many-cylinder'd steam printing-press – See, the electric
      telegraph, stretching across the Continent, from the
      Western Sea to Manhattan;
See, through Atlantica's depths, pulses American, Europe
      reaching – pulses of Europe, duly return'd;
See, the strong and quick locomotive, as it departs, panting,
      blowing the steam-whistle;
See, ploughmen, ploughing farms – See, miners, digging
      mines – See, the numberless factories;
See, mechanics, busy at their benches, with tools – See from
      among them, superior judges, philosophs, Presidents,
      emerge, drest in working dresses;
See, lounging through the shops and fields of The States, me,
      well-belov'd, close-held by day and night;
Hear the loud echoes of my songs there! Read the hints
      come at last.

20

O Camerado close!
O you and me at last – and us two only.

O a word to clear one's path ahead endlessly!
O something extatic and undemonstrable! O music wild!
O now I triumph—and you shall also;
O hand in hand—O wholesome pleasure—O one more desirer
        and lover!
O to haste, firm holding—to haste, haste on with me.

WALT WHITMAN (SONG OF MYSELF)

First published in 1855

1

I CELEBRATE MYSELF;
And what I assume you shall assume;
For every atom belonging to me, as good belongs to you.

I loafe and invite my Soul;
I lean and loafe at my ease, observing a spear of summer grass.

Houses and rooms are full of perfumes—the shelves are
        crowded with perfumes;
I breathe the fragrance myself, and know it and like it;
The distillation would intoxicate me also, but I shall not let it.

The atmosphere is not a perfume—it has no taste of the
        distillation—it is odorless;
It is for my mouth forever—I am in love with it;
I will go to the bank by the wood, and become undisguised
        and naked;
I am mad for it to be in contact with me.

2

The smoke of my own breath;
Echoes, ripples, buzz'd whispers, love-root, silk-thread,
    crotch and vine;
My respiration and inspiration, the beating of my heart, the
    passing of blood and air through my lungs;
The sniff of green leaves and dry leaves, and of the shore, and
    dark-color'd sea-rocks, and of hay in the barn;
The sound of the belch'd words of my voice, words loos'd to
    the eddies of the wind;
A few light kisses, a few embraces, a reaching around of arms;
The play of shine and shade on the trees as the supple
    boughs wag;
The delight alone, or in the rush of the streets, or along the
    fields and hill-sides;
The feeling of health, the full-noon trill, the song of me rising
    from bed and meeting the sun.

Have you reckon'd a thousand acres much? have you reckon'd
    the earth much?
Have you practis'd so long to learn to read?
Have you felt so proud to get at the meaning of poems?

Stop this day and night with me, and you shall possess the
    origin of all poems;
You shall possess the good of the earth and sun – (there are
    millions of suns left;)
You shall no longer take things at second or third hand, nor
    look through the eyes of the dead, nor feed on the
    spectres in books;

You shall not look through my eyes either, nor take things
        from me:
You shall listen to all sides, and filter them from yourself.

3

I have heard what the talkers were talking, the talk of the
        beginning and the end;
But I do not talk of the beginning or the end.

There was never any more inception than there is now,
Nor any more youth or age than there is now;
And will never be any more perfection than there is now,
Nor any more heaven or hell than there is now.
Urge, and urge, and urge;
Always the procreant urge of the world.

Out of the dimness opposite equals advance—always substance
        and increase, always sex;
Always a knit of identity—always distinction—always a breed
        of life.

To elaborate is no avail—learn'd and unlearn'd feel that it is so.

Sure as the most certain sure, plumb in the uprights, well
        entretied, braced in the beams,
Stout as a horse, affectionate, haughty, electrical,
I and this mystery, here we stand.

Clear and sweet is my Soul, and clear and sweet is all that is
        not my Soul.

Lack one lacks both, and the unseen is proved by the seen,
Till that becomes unseen, and receives proof in its turn.

Showing the best, and dividing it from the worst,
          age vexes age;
Knowing the perfect fitness and equanimity of things,
          while they discuss I am silent, and go bathe and
          admire myself.

Welcome is every organ and attribute of me, and of any man
          hearty and clean;
Not an inch, nor a particle of an inch, is vile, and none shall
          be less familiar than the rest.

I am satisfied—I see, dance, laugh, sing:
As the hugging and loving Bed-fellow sleeps at my side
          through the night, and withdraws at the peep of the
          day, with stealthy tread,
Leaving me baskets cover'd with white towels, swelling the
          house with their plenty,
Shall I postpone my acceptation and realization, and scream at
          my eyes,
That they turn from gazing after and down the road,
And forthwith cipher and show me a cent,
Exactly the contents of one, and exactly the contents of two,
          and which is ahead?

4

Trippers and askers surround me;
People I meet—the effect upon me of my early life, or the ward
          and city I live in, or the nation,

The latest dates, discoveries, inventions, societies, authors old
  and new,
My dinner, dress, associates, looks, compliments, dues,
The real or fancied indifference of some man or woman I love,
The sickness of one of my folds, or of myself, or ill-doing, or
  loss or lack of money, or depressions or exaltations;
Battles, the horrors of fratricidal war, the fever of doubtful
  news, the fitful events;
These come to me days and nights, and go from me again,
But they are not the Me myself.

Apart from the pulling and hauling stands what I am;
Stands amused, complacent, compassionating, idle, unitary;
Looks down, is erect, or bends an arm on an impalpable
  certain rest,
Looking with side-curved head, curious what will come next;
Both in and out of the game, and watching and wondering at it.

Backward I see in my own days where I sweated through fog
  with linguists and contenders;
I have no mockings or arguments—I witness and wait.

5

I believe in you, my Soul—the other I am must not abase
  itself to you;
And you must not be abased to the other.
Loafe with me on the grass—loose the stop from your throat;
Not words, not music or rhyme I want—not custom or lecture,
  not even the best;
Only the lull I like, the hum of your valved voice.

I mind how once we lay, such a transparent summer morning;
How you settled your head athwart my hips, and gently turn'd
          over upon me,
And parted the shirt from my bosom-bone, and plunged your
          tongue to my bare-stript heart,
And reach'd till you felt my beard, and reach'd till you held
          my feet.

Swiftly arose and spread around me the peace and knowledge
          that pass all the argument of the earth;
And I know that the hand of God is the promise of my own,
And I know that the spirit of God is the brother of my own;
And that all the men ever born are also my brothers, and the
          women my sisters and lovers;
And that a kelson of the creation is love;
And limitless are leaves, stiff or drooping in the fields;
And brown ants in the little wells beneath them;
And mossy scabs of the worm fence, and heap'd stones, elder,
          mullen and poke-weed.

6

A child said, *What is the grass?* fetching it to me with full
          hands;
How could I answer the child? I do not know what it is, any
          more than he.

I guess it must be the flag of my disposition, out of hopeful
          green stuff woven.

Or I guess it is the handkerchief of the Lord,
A scented gift and remembrancer, designedly dropt,

Bearing the owner's name someway in the corners, that we may
      see and remark, and say, *Whose?*

Or I guess the grass is itself a child, the produced babe
      of the vegetation.

Or I guess it is a uniform hieroglyphic;
And it means, Sprouting alike in broad zones and narrow zones,
Growing among black folks as among white;
Kanuck, Tuckahoe, Congressman, Cuff, I give them the same, I
      receive them the same.

And now it seems to me the beautiful uncut hair of graves.

Tenderly will I use you, curling grass;
It may be you transpire from the breasts of young men;
It may be if I had known them I would have loved them;
It may be you are from old people, and from women, and from
      offspring taken soon out of their mothers' laps;
And here you are the mothers' laps.

This grass is very dark to be from the white heads of
      old mothers;
Darker than the colorless beards of old men;
Dark to come from under the faint red roofs of mouths.

O I perceive after all so many uttering tongues!
And I perceive they do not come from the roofs of mouths
      for nothing.

I wish I could translate the hints about the dead young men
        and women,
And the hints about old men and mothers, and the offspring
        taken soon out of their laps.

What do you think has become of the young and old men?
And what do you think has become of the women and
        children?

They are alive and well somewhere;
The smallest sprout shows there is really no death;
And if ever there was, it led forward life, and does not wait at
        the end to arrest it,
And ceas'd the moment life appear'd.

All goes onward and outward—nothing collapses;
And to die is different from what any one supposed,
        and luckier.

7

Has any one supposed it lucky to be born?
I hasten to inform him or her, it is just as lucky to die, and I
        know it.

I pass death with the dying, and birth with the new-wash'd
        babe, and am not contain'd between my hat and boots;
And peruse manifold objects, no two alike, and every one
        good;
The earth good, and the stars good, and their adjuncts all
        good.

I am not an earth, nor an adjunct of an earth;
I am the mate and companion of people, all just as immortal
        and fathomless as myself;
(They do not know how immortal, but I know.)

Every kind for itself and its own—for me mine, male
        and female;
For me those that have been boys, and that love women;
For me the man that is proud, and feels how it stings
        to be slighted;
For me the sweet-heart and the old maid—for me mothers, and
        the mothers of mothers;
For me lips that have smiled, eyes that have shed tears;
For me children, and the begetters of children.

Undrape! you are not guilty to me, nor stale, nor discarded;
I see through the broadcloth and gingham, whether or no;
And am around, tenacious, acquisitive, tireless, and cannot be
        shaken away.

8

The little one sleeps in its cradle;
I lift the gauze, and look a long time, and silently brush away
        flies with my hand.

The youngster and the red-faced girl turn aside up the
        bushy hill;
I peeringly view them from the top.
The suicide sprawls on the bloody floor of the bed-room;
I witness the corpse with its dabbled hair—I note where the
        pistol has fallen.

The blab of the pave, the tires of carts, sluff of boot-soles, talk
of the promenaders;
The heavy omnibus, the driver with his interrogating thumb,
the clank of the shod horses on the granite floor;
The snow-sleighs, the clinking, shouted jokes, pelts of
snow-balls;
The hurrahs for popular favorites, the fury of rous'd mobs;
The flap of the curtain'd litter, a sick man inside, borne
to the hospital;
The meeting of enemies, the sudden oath, the blows and fall;
The excited crowd,m the policeman with his star, quickly
working his passage to the centre of the crowd;
The impassive stones that receive and return so many echoes;
What groans of over-fed or half-starv'd who fall sun-struck, or
in fits;
What exclamations of women taken suddenly, who hurry
home and give birth to babes;
What living and buried speech is always vibrating here—what
howls restrain'd by decorum;
Arrests of criminals, slights, adulterous offers made,
acceptances, rejections with convex lips;
I mind them or the show or resonance of them—I come,
and I depart.

9

The big doors of the country barn stand open and ready;
The dried grass of the harvest-time loads the slow-drawn wagon;
The clear light plays on the brown gray and green intertinged;
The armfuls are pack'd to the sagging mow.
I am there—I help—I came stretch'd atop of the load;

I felt its soft jolts – one leg reclined on the other;
I jump from the cross-beams, and seize the clover and timothy,
And roll head over heels, and tangle my hair full of wisps.

10

Alone, far in the wilds and mountains, I hunt,
Wandering, amazed at my own lightness and glee;
In the late afternoon choosing a safe spot to pass the night,
Kindling a fire and broiling the fresh-kill'd game;
Falling asleep on the gather'd leaves, with my dog and gun by
        my side.

The Yankee clipper is under her sky-sails – she cuts the sparkle
        and scud;
My eyes settle the land – I bend at her prow, or shout joyously
        from the deck.

The boatmen and clam-diggers arose early and stopt for me;
I tuck'd my trowser-ends in my boots, and went and had a
        good time:
(You should have been with us that day round the
        chowder-kettle.)

I saw the marriage of the trapper in the open air in the far
        west – the bride was a red girl;
Her father and his friends sat near, cross-legged and dumbly
        smoking – they had moccasins to their feet, and large
        thick blankets hanging from their shoulders;
On a bank lounged the trapper – he was drest mostly in
        skins – his luxuriant beard and curls protected his
        neck – he held his bride by the hand;

She had long eyelashes – her head was bare – her coarse straight
      locks descended upon her voluptuous limbs and
      reach'd to her feet.

The runaway slave came to my house and stopt outside;
I heard his motions crackling the twigs of the woodpile;
Through the swung half-door of the kitchen I saw him limpsy
      and weak,
And went where he sat on a log, and led him in and
      assured him,
And brought water, and fill'd a tub for his sweated body
      and bruis'd feet,
And gave him a room that enter'd from my own, and gave him
      some coarse clean clothes,
And remember perfectly well his revolving eyes and his
      awkwardness,
And remember putting plasters on the galls of his neck
      and ankles;
He staid with me a week before he was recuperated and
      pass'd north;
(I had him sit next me at table – my fire-lock lean'd in the corner.)

11

Twenty-eight young men bathe by the shore;
Twenty-eight young men, and all so friendly:
Twenty-eight years of womanly life, and all so lonesome.

She owns the fine house by the rise of the bank;
She hides, handsome and richly drest, aft the blinds
      of the window.

Which of the young men does she like the best?
Ah, the homeliest of them is beautiful to her.

Where are you off to, lady? for I see you;
You splash in the water there, yet stay stock still in your room.

Dancing and laughing along the beach came the
        twenty-ninth bather;
The rest did not see her, but she saw them and loved them.

The beards of the young men glisten'd with wet, it ran from
        their long hair:
Little streams pass'd all over their bodies.

An unseen hand also pass'd over their bodies;
It descended tremblingly from their temples and ribs.

The young men float on their backs—their white bellies bulge
        to the sun—they do not ask who seizes fast to them;
They do not know who puffs and declines with pendant and
        bending arch;
They do not think whom they souse with spray.

12

The butcher-boy puts off his killing clothes, or sharpens his
        knife at the stall in the market;
I loiter, enjoying his repartee, and his shuffle and break-down.

Blacksmiths with grimed and hairy chests environ the anvil;
Each has his main-sledge—they are all out—(there is a great
        heat in the fire.)

From the cinder-strew'd threshold I follow their movements;
The lithe sheer of their waists plays even with their
        massive arms;

Over-hand the hammers swing–over-hand so slow–over-hand
      so sure:
They do not hasten–each man hits in his place.

13

The negro holds firmly the reins of his four horses–the block
      swags underneath on its tied-over chain;
The negro that drives the dray of the stone-yard–steady and
      tall he stands, pois'd on one leg on the string-piece;
His blue shirt exposes his ample neck and breast, and loosens
      over his hip-band;
His glance is calm and commanding–he tosses the slouch of
      his hat away from his forehead;
The sun falls on his crispy hair and moustache–falls on the
      black of his polish'd and perfect limbs.

I behold the picturesque giant, and love him–and I do not
      stop there;
I go with the team also.

In me the caresser of life wherever moving–backward as well
      as forward slueing;
To niches aside and junior bending.

Oxen that rattle the yoke and chain, or halt in the leafy shade!
      what is that you express in your eyes?
It seems to me more than all the print I have read in my life.

My trend scares the wood-drake and wood-duck, on my
      distant and day-long ramble;
They rise together–they slowly circle around.

I believe in those wing'd purposes,
And acknowledge red, yellow, white, playing within me,
And consider green and violet, and the tufted crown,
          intentional;
And do not call the tortoise unworthy because she is not
          something else;
And the jay in the woods never studied the gamut, yet trills
          pretty well to me;
And the look of the bay mare shames silliness out of me.

14

The wild gander leads his flock through the cool night;
Ya-honk! he says, and sounds it down to me like an invitation;
(The pert may suppose it meaningless, but I listen close;
I find its purpose and place up there toward the wintry sky.)

The sharp-hoof'd moose of the north, the cat on the house-sill,
          the chickadee, the prairie-dog,
The litter of the grunting sow as they tug at her teats,
The brood of the turkey-hen, and she with her half-spread wings;
I see in them and myself the same old law.

The press of my foot to the earth springs a hundred affections;
They scorn the best I can do to relate them.

I am enamour'd of growing out-doors,
Of men that live among cattle, or taste of the ocean or woods,
Of the builders and steerers of ships, and the wielders of axes
          and mauls, and the drivers of horses;
I can eat and sleep with them week in and week out.

What is commonest, cheapest, nearest, easiest, is Me;
Me going in for my chances, spending for vast returns;
Adorning myself to bestow myself on the first that
          will take me;
Not asking the sky to come down to my good will;
Scattering it freely forever.

15

The pure contralto sings in the organ loft;
The carpenter dresses his plank—the tongue of his foreplane
          whistles its wild ascending lisp;
The married and unmarried children ride home to their
          Thanksgiving dinner;
The pilot seizes the king-pin—he heaves down with a
          strong arm;
The mate stands braced in the whale-boat—lance and harpoon
          are ready;
The duck-shooter walks by silent and cautious stretches;
The deacons are ordain'd with cross'd hands at the altar;
The spinning-girl retreats and advances to the hum of
          the big wheel;
The farmer stops by the bars, as he walks on a First-day loafe,
          and looks at the oats and rye;
The lunatic is carried at last to the asylum, a confirm'd case,
(He will never sleep any more as he did in the cot in his
          mother's bed-room;)
The jour printer with gray head and gaunt jaws works
          at his case,
He turns his quid of tobacco, while his eyes blurr with
          the manuscript;
The malform'd limbs are tied to the surgeon's table,

What is removed drops horribly in a pail;
The quadroon girl is sold at the auction-stand – the drunkard
          nods by the bar-room stove;
The machinist rolls up his sleeves – the policeman travels his
          beat – the gate-keeper marks who pass;
The young fellow drives the express-wagon – (I love him,
          though I do not know him;)
The half-breed straps on his light boots to compete
          in the race;
The western turkey-shooting draws old and young – some lean
          on their rifles, some sit on logs,
Out from the crowd steps the marksman, takes his position,
          levels his piece;
The groups of newly-come immigrants cover the wharf
          or levee;
As the woolly-pates hoe in the sugar-field, the overseer views
          them from his saddle;
The bugle calls in the ball-room, the gentlemen run for their
          partners, the dancers bow to each other;
The youth lies awake in the cedar-roof'd garret, and harks to
          the musical rain;
The Wolverine sets traps on the creek that helps fill
          the Huron;
The squaw, wrapt in her yellow-hemm'd cloth, is offering
          moccasins and bead-bags for sale;
The connoisseur peers along the exhibition-gallery with half-
          shut eyes bent sideways;
As the deck-hands make fast the steamboat, the plank is
          thrown for the shore-going passengers;
The young sister holds out the skein, while the elder sister
          winds it off in a ball, and stops now and then
          for the knots;

The one-year wife is recovering and happy, having a week ago
    borne her first child;
The clean-hair'd Yankee girl works with her sewing-machine,
    or in the factory or mill;
The nine months' gone is in the parturition chamber, her
    faintness and pains are advancing;
The paving-man leans on his two-handed rammer–the
    reporter's lead flies swiftly over the note-book–the
    sign-painter is lettering with red and gold;
The canal boy trots on the tow-path–the book-keeper counts
    at his desk–the shoemaker waxes his thread;
The conductor beats time for the band, and all the performers
    follow him;
The child is baptized–the convert is making his first
    professions;
The regatta is spread on the bay–the race is begun–how the
    white sails sparkle!
The drover, watching his drove, sings out to them that
    would stray;
The pedler sweats with his pack on his back, (the purchaser
    higgling about the odd cent;)
The camera and plate are prepared, the lady must sit for
    her daguerreotype;
The bride unrumples her white dress, the minute-hand of the
    clock moves slowly;
The opium-eater reclines with rigid head and just-open'd lips;
The prostitute draggles her shawl, her bonnet bobs on her
    tipsy and pimpled neck;
The crowd laugh at her blackguard oaths, the men jeer and
    wink to each other;
(Miserable! I do not laugh at your oaths, nor jeer you;)

The President, holding a cabinet council, is surrounded by the
        Great Secretaries;
On the piazza walk three matrons stately and friendly with
        twined arms;
The crew of the fish-smack pack repeated layers of halibut in
        the hold;
The Missourian crosses the plains, toting his wares and
        his cattle;
As the fare-collector goes through the train, he gives notice by
        the jingling of loose change;
The floor-men are laying the floor—the tinners are tinning the
        roof—the masons are calling for mortar;
In single file, each shouldering his hod, pass onward
        the laborers;
Seasons pursuing each other, the indescribable crowd is
        gather'd—it is the Fourth of Seventh-month— (What
        salutes of cannon and small arms!)
Seasons pursuing each other, the plougher ploughs, the mower
        mows, and the winter-grain falls in the ground.
Off on the lakes the pike-fisher watches and waits by the hold
        in the frozen surface;
The stumps stand thick round the clearing, the squatter strikes
        deep with his axe;
Flatboatmen make fast, towards dusk, near the cottonwood
        or pekan-trees;
Coon-seekers go through the regions of the Red river, or
        through those drain'd by the Tennessee, or through
        those of the Arkansaw;
Torches shine in the dark that hangs on the Chattahoochee
        or Altamahaw;
Patriarchs sit at supper with sons and grandsons and great-
        grandsons around them;

In walls of adobie, in canvas tents, rest hunters and trappers
     after their day's sport;
The city sleeps, and the country sleeps;
The living sleep for their time, the dead sleep for their time;
The old husband sleeps by his wife, and the young husband
     sleeps by his wife;
And these one and all tend inward to me, and I tend outward
     to them;
And such as it is to be of these, more or less, I am.

16

I am of old and young, of the foolish as much as the wise;
Regardless of others, ever regardful of others,
Maternal as well as paternal, a child as well as a man,
Stuff'd with the stuff that is coarse, and stuff'd with the stuff
     that is fine;
One of the Great Nation, the nation of many nations, the
     smallest the same, and the largest the same;
A southerner soon as a northerner – a planter nonchalant and
     hospitable, down by the Oconee I live;
A Yankee, bound by my own way, ready for trade, my joints
     the limberest joints on earth, and the sternest joints
     on earth;
A Kentuckian, walking the vale of the Elkhorn, in my deer-
     skin leggings – a Louisianian or Georgian;
A boatman over lakes or bays, or along coasts – a Hoosier,
     Badger, Buckeye;
At home on Kanadian snow-shoes, or up in the bush, or with
     fishermen off Newfoundland;
At home in the fleet of ice-boats, sailing with the rest
     and tacking;

At home on the hills of Vermont, or in the woods of Maine, or
        the Texan ranch;
Comrade of Californians – comrade of free north-westerners,
        (loving their big proportions;)
Comrade of raftsmen and coalmen – comrade of all who shake
        hands and welcome to drink and meat;
A learner with the simplest, a teacher of the thoughtfullest;
A novice beginning, yet experient of myriads of seasons;
Of every hue and caste am I, of every rank and religion;
A farmer, mechanic, artist, gentleman, sailor, quaker;
A prisoner, fancy-man, rowdy, lawyer, physician, priest.

I resist anything better than my own diversity;
I breathe the air, but leave plenty after me,
And am not stuck up, and am in my place.

(The moth and the fish-eggs are in their place;
The suns I see, and the suns I cannot see, are in their place;
The palpable is in its place, and the impalpable is in its place.)

17

These are the thoughts of all men in all ages and lands – they
        are not original with me;
If they are not yours as much as mine, they are nothing, or
        next to nothing;
If they are not the riddle, and the untying of the riddle, they
        are nothing;
If they are not just as close as they are distant, they
        are nothing.

This is the grass that grows wherever the land is, and
          the water is;
This is the common air that bathes the globe.

18

With music strong I come—with my cornets and my drums,
I play not marches for accepted victors only—I play great
          marches for conquer'd and slain persons.

Have you heard that it was good to gain the day?
I also say it is good to fall—battles are lost in the same spirit in
          which they are won.

I beat and pound for the dead;
I blow through my embouchures my loudest and gayest for them.

Vivas to those who have fail'd!
And to those whose war-vessels sank in the sea!
And to those themselves who sank in the sea!
And to all generals that lost engagements! and all
          overcome heroes!
And the numberless unknown heroes, equal to the greatest
          heroes known.

19

This is the meal equally set—this is the meat for
          natural hunger;
It is for the wicked just the same as the righteous—I make
          appointments with all;
I will not have a single person slighted or left away;
The kept-woman, sponger, thief, are hereby invited;
The heavy-lipp'd slave is invited—the venerealee is invited:
There shall be no difference between them and the rest.

This is the press of a bashful hand—this is the float and
       odor of hair;
This is the touch of my lips to yours—this is the murmur
       of yearning;
This is the far-off depth and height reflecting my own face;
This is the thoughtful merge of myself, and the outlet again.

Do you guess I have some intricate purpose?
Well, I have—for the Fourth-month showers have, and the mica
       on the side of a rock has.

Do you take it I would astonish?
Does the daylight astonish? Does the early redstart, twittering
       through the woods?
Do I astonish more than they?

This hour I tell things in confidence;
I might not tell everybody, but I will tell you.

20

Who goes there? hankering, gross, mystical, nude;
How is it I extract strength from the beef I eat?

What is a man, anyhow? What am I? What are you?

All I mark as my own, you shall offset it with your own;
Else it were time lost listening to me.

I do not snivel that snivel the world over,
That months are vacuums, and the ground but wallow and
       filth;

That life is a suck and a sell, and nothing remains at the end
    but threadbare crape, and tears.

Whimpering and truckling fold with powders for invalids—
    conformity goes to the fourth-remov'd;
I wear my hat as I please, indoors or out.

Why should I pray? Why should I venerate and be
    ceremonious?

Having pried through the strata, analyzed to a hair, counsell'd
    with doctors, and calculated close,
I find no sweeter fat than sticks to my own bones.

In all people I see myself—none more, and not one a barley-
    corn less;
And the good or bad I say of myself, I say of them.

And I know I am solid and sound;
To me the converging objects of the universe perpetually flow;
All are written to me, and I must get what the writing means.

I know I am deathless;
I know this orbit of mine cannot be swept by the
    carpenter's compass;
I know I shall not pass like a child's carlacue cut with a
    burnt stick at night.

I know I am august;
I do not trouble my spirit to vindicate itself or be understood;

I see that the elementary laws never apologize;
(I reckon I behave no prouder than the level I plant my house
        by, after all.)

I exist as I am – that is enough;
If no other in the world be aware, I sit content;
And if each and all be aware, I sit content.

One world is aware, and by far the largest to me, and that
        is myself;
And whether I come to my own to-day, or in ten thousand or
        ten million years,
I can cheerfully take it now, or with equal cheerfulness
        I can wait.

My foothold is tenon'd and mortis'd in granite;
I laugh at what you call dissolution;
And I know the amplitude of time.

21

I am the poet of the Body;
And I am the poet of the Soul.

The pleasures of heaven are with me, and the pains of hell are
        with me;
The first I graft and increase upon myself – the latter I translate
        into a new tongue.

I am the poet of the woman the same as the man;
And I say it is as great to be a woman as to be a man;
And I say there is nothing greater than the mother of men.

I chant the chant of dilation or pride;
We have had ducking and deprecating about enough;
I show that size is only development.

Have you outstript the rest? Are you the President?
It is a trifle – they will more than arrive there, every one, and
     still pass on.

I am he that walks with the tender and growing night;
I call to the earth and sea, half-held by the night.

Press close, bare-bosom'd night! Press close, magnetic,
     nourishing night!
Night of south winds! night of the large few stars!
Still, nodding night! mad, naked, summer night.

Smile, O voluptuous, cool-breath'd earth!
Earth of the slumbering and liquid trees;
Earth of departed sunset! earth of the mountains, misty-topt!
Earth of the vitreous pour of the full moon, just tinged
     with blue!
Earth of shine and dark, mottling the tide of the river!
Earth of the limpid gray of clouds, brighter and clearer
     for my sake!
Far-swooping elbow'd earth! rich, apple-blossom'd earth!
Smile, for your lover comes!

Prodigal, you have given me love! Therefore I to you give love!
O unspeakable, passionate love!

22

You sea! I resign myself to you also–I guess what you mean;
I behold from the beach your crooked inviting fingers;
I believe you refuse to go back without feeling of me;
We must have a turn together–I undress–hurry me out of
      sight of the land;
Cushion me soft, rock me in billowy drowse;
Dash me with amorous wet–I can repay you.

Sea of stretch'd ground-swells!
Sea breathing broad and convulsive breaths!
Sea of the brine of life! sea of unshovell'd yet
      always-ready graves!
Howler and scooper of storms! capricious and dainty sea!
I am integral with you–I too am of one phase, and
      of all phases.

Partaker of influx and efflux I–extoller of hate
      and conciliation;
Extoller of amies, and those that sleep in each others' arms.

I am he attesting sympathy;
(Shall I make my list of things in the house, and skip the
      house that supports them?)

I am not the poet of goodness only–I do not decline to be the
      poet of wickedness also.

Washes and razors for foofoos–for me freckles and a
      bristling beard.

What blurt is this about virtue and about vice?
Evil propels me, and reform of evil propels me—I
      stand indifferent;
My gait is no fault-finder's or rejecter's gait;
I moisten the roots of all that has grown.

Did you fear some scrofula out of the unflagging pregnancy?
Did you guess the celestial laws are yet to be work'd over
      and rectified?

I find one side a balance, and the antipodal side a balance;
Soft doctrine as steady help as stable doctrine;
Thoughts and deeds of the present, our rouse and early start.

This minute that comes to me over the past decillions,
There is no better than it and now.

What behaved well in the past, or behaves well to-day, is not
      such a wonder;
The wonder is, always and always, how there can be a mean
      man or an infidel.

23

Endless unfolding of words of ages!
And mine a word of the modern—the word En-Masse.

A word of the faith that never balks;
Here or henceforward, it is all the same to me—I accept
      Time, absolutely.

It alone is without flaw—it rounds and completes all;
That mystic, baffling wonder I love, alone completes all.

I accept reality, and dare not question it;
Materialism first and last imbuing.

Hurrah for positive science! long live exact demonstration!
Fetch stonecrop, mixt with cedar and branches of lilac;
This is the lexicographer – this the chemist – this made a
          grammar of the old cartouches;
These mariners put the ship through dangerous unknown seas;
This is the geologist – this works with the scalpel – and this is a
          mathematician.

Gentlemen! to you the first honors always:
Your facts are useful and real – and yet they are not
          my dwelling;
(I but enter by them to an area of my dwelling.)

Less the reminders of properties told, my words;
And more the reminders, they, of life untold, and of freedom
          and extrication,
And make short account of neuters and geldings, and favor
          men and women fully equipt,
And beat the gong of revolt, and stop with fugitives, and them
          that plot and conspire.

24

Walt Whitman am I, a Kosmos, of mighty Manhattan the son,
Turbulent, fleshy and sensual, eating, drinking and breeding;
No sentimentalist – no stander above men and women, or apart
          from them;
No more modest than immodest.

Unscrew the locks from the doors!
Unscrew the doors themselves from their jambs!

Whoever degrades another degrades me;
And whatever is done or said returns at last to me.

Through me the afflatus surging and surging – through me the
      current and index.

I speak the pass-word primeval – I give the sign of democracy;
By God! I will accept nothing which all cannot have their
      counterpart of on the same terms.

Through me many long dumb voices;
Voices of the interminable generations of slaves;
Voices of prostitutes, and of deform;d persons;
Voices of the diseas'd and despairing, and of thieves
      and dwarfs;
Voices of cycles of preparation and accretion,
And of the threads that connect the stars – and of wombs, and
      of the father-stuff,
And of the rights of them the others are down upon;
Of the trivial, flat, foolish, despised,
Fog in the air, beetles rolling balls of dung.

Through me forbidden voices;
Voice of sexes and lusts – voices veil'd, and I remove the veil;
Voices indecent, by me clarified and transfigur'd.

I do not press my fingers across my mouth;
I keep as delicate around the bowels as around the head
      and heart;
Copulation is no more rank to me than death is.

I believe in the flesh and the appetites;
Seeing, hearing, feeling, are miracles, and each part and tag of
    me is a miracle.

Divine am I inside and out, and I make holy whatever I touch
    or am touch'd from;
The scent of these arm-pits, aroma finer than prayer;
This head more than churches, bibles, and all the creeds.

If I worship one thing more than another, it shall be the
    spread of my own body, or any part of it.

Translucent mould of me, it shall be you!
Shaded ledges and rests, it shall be you!
Firm masculine colter, it shall be you.

Whatever goes to the tilth of me, it shall be you!
You my rich blood! Your milky stream, pale strippings of
    my life.

Breast that presses against other breasts, it shall be you!
My brain, it shall be your occult convolutions.

Root of wash'd sweet flag! timorous pond-snipe! nest of
    guarded duplicate eggs! it shall be you!
Mix'd tussled hay of head, beard, brawn, it shall be you!
Trickling sap of maple! fibre of manly wheat! it shall be you!

Sun so generous, it shall be you!
Vapors lighting and shading my face, it shall be you!
You sweaty brooks and dews, it shall be you!
Winds whose soft-tickling genitals rub against me, it
    shall be you!

Broad, muscular fields! branches of live oak! loving lounger in
my winding paths! it shall be you!
Hands I have taken – face I have kiss'd – mortal I have ever
touch'd! it shall be you.

I dote on myself – there is that lot of me, and all so luscious;
Each moment, and whatever happens, thrills me with joy.

O I am wonderful!
I cannot tell how my ankles bend, nor whence the cause of my
faintest wish;
Nor the cause of the friendship I emit, nor the cause of the
friendship I take again.

That I walk up my stoop! I pause to consider if it really be;
A morning-glory at my window satisfies me more than the
metaphysics of books.

To behold the day-break!
The little light fades the immense and diaphanous shadows;
The air tastes good to my palate.

Hefts of the moving world, at innocent gambols, silently rising,
freshly exuding,
Scooting obliquely high and low.

Something I cannot see puts upward libidinous prongs;
Seas of bright juice suffuse heaven.

The earth by the sky staid with – the daily close of
          their junction;
The heav'd challenge from the east that moment over my head;
The mocking taunt, See then whether you shall be master!

25

Dazzling and tremendous, how quick the sun-rise would
          kill me,
If I could not now and always send sun-rise out of me.

We also ascend, dazzling and tremendous as the sun;
We found our own, O my Soul, in the calm and cool of
          the daybreak.

My voice goes after what my eyes cannot reach;
With the twirl of my tongue I encompass worlds, and volumes
          of worlds.

Speech is the twin of my vision – it is unequal to
          measure itself;
It provokes me forever;
It says sarcastically, *Walt, you contain enough – why don't you let
          it out, then?*

Come now, I will not be tantalized – you conceive too much of
          articulation.

Do you not know, O speech, how the buds beneath you
          are folded?
Waiting in gloom, protected by frost;
The dirt receding before my prophetical screams;
I underlying causes, to balance them at last;

My knowledge my live parts – it keeping tally with the meaning
        of things,
HAPPINESS – which, whoever hears me, let him or her set out in
        search of this day.

My final merit I refuse you – I refuse putting from me what I
        really am;
Encompass worlds, but never try to encompass me;
I crowd your sleekest and best by simply looking toward you.

Writing and talk do not prove me;
I carry the plenum of proof, and everything else, in my face;
With the hush of my lips I wholly confound the skeptic.

26

I think I will do nothing now but listen,
To accrue what I hear into myself – to let sounds contribute
        toward me.

I hear bravuras of birds, bustle of growing wheat, gossip of
        flames, clack of sticks cooking my meals;
I hear the sound I love, the sound of the human voice;
I hear all sounds running together, combined, fused
        or following;
Sounds of the city, and sounds out of the city – sounds of the
        day and night;
Talkative young ones to those that like them – the loud laugh
        of work-people at their meals;
The angry base of disjointed friendship – the faint tones
        of the sick;
The judge with hands tight to the desk, his pallid lips
        pronouncing a death-sentence;

The heave'e'yo of stevedores unlading ships by the wharves—
        the refrain of the anchor-lifters;
The ring of alarm-bells—the cry of fire—the whirr of swift-
        streaking engines and hose-carts, with premonitory
        tinkles, and color'd lights;
The steam-whistle—the solid roll of the train of approaching cars;
The slow-march play'd at the head of the association,
        marching two and two,
(They go to guard some corpse—the flag tops are draped with
        black muslin.)

I hear the violoncello ('tis the young man's heart's complaint;)
I hear the key'd cornet—it glides quickly in through my ears;
It shakes mad-sweet pangs through my belly and breast.

I hear the chorus—it is a grand opera;
Ah, this indeed is music! This suits me.

A tenor large and fresh as the creation fills me;
The orbic flex of his mouth is pouring and filling me full.

I hear the train'd soprano—(what work, with hers, is this?)
The orchestra whirls me wider than Uranus flies;
It wrenches such ardors from me, I did not know I
        possess'd them;
It sails me—I dab with bare feet—they are lick'd by the
        indolent waves;
I am exposed, cut by bitter and angry hail—I lose my breath,
Steep'd amid honey'd morphine, my windpipe throttled in
        fakes of death;

At length let up again to feel the puzzle of puzzles,
And that we call BEING.

27

To be, in any form—what is that?
(Round and round we go, all of us, and ever come
        back thither;)
If nothing lay more develop'd, the quahaug in its callous shell
        were enough.

Mine is no callous shell;
I have instant conductors all over me, whether I pass or stop;
They seize every object and lead it harmlessly through me.

I merely stir, press, feel with my fingers, and am happy;
To touch my person to some one else's is about as much as I
        can stand.

28

Is this then a touch? quivering me to a new identity,
Flames and ether making a rush for my veins,
Treacherous tip of me reaching and crowding to help them,
My flesh and blood playing out lightning to strike what is
        hardly different from myself;
On all sides prurient provokers stiffening my limbs,
Straining the udder of my heart for its withheld drip,
Behaving licentious toward me, taking no denial,
Depriving me of my best, as for a purpose,
Unbuttoning my clothes, holding me by the bare waist,
Deluding my confusion with the calm of the sunlight and
        pasture-fields,
Immodestly sliding the fellow-senses away,

They bribed to swap off with touch, and go and graze at the
      edges of me;
No consideration, no regard for my draining strength or
      my anger;
Fetching the rest of the herd around to enjoy them a while,
Then all uniting to stand on a headland and worry me.

The sentries desert every other part of me;
They have left me helpless to a red marauder;
They all come to the headland, to witness and assist
      against me.

I am given up by traitors;
I talk wildly–I have lost my wits–I and nobody else am the
      greatest traitor;
I went myself first to the headland–my own hands carried me
      there.

You villian touch! what are you doing? My breath is tight
      in its throat;
Unclench your floodgates! you are too much for me.

29

Blind, loving, wrestling touch! sheath'd, hooded,
      sharp-tooth'd touch!
Did it make you ache so, leaving me?

Parting, track'd by arriving–perpetual payment of
      perpetual loan;
Rich, showering rain, and recompense richer afterward.

Sprouts take and accumulate – stand by the curb prolific
        and vital:
Landscapes, projected, masculine, full-sized and golden.

30

All truths wait in all things;
They neither hasten their own delivery, nor resist it;
They do not need the obstetric forceps of the surgeon;
The insignificant is as big to me as any;
(What is less or more than a touch?)

Logic and sermons never convince;
The damp of the night drives deeper into my soul.

Only what proves itself to every man and woman is so;
Only what nobody denies is so.

A minute and a drop of me settle my brain;
I believe the soggy clods shall become lovers and lamps,
And a compend of compends is the meat of a man or woman,
And a summit and flower there is the feeling they have for
        each other,
And they are to branch boundlessly out of that lesson until it
        becomes omnific,
And until every one shall delight us, and we them.

31

I believe a leaf of grass is no less than the journey-work
        of the stars,
And the pismire is equally perfect, and a grain of sand, and
        the egg of the wren,

And the tree-toad is a chef-d'œuvre for the highest,
And the running blackberry would adorn the parlors
      of heaven,
And the narrowest hinge in my hand puts to scorn
      all machinery,
And the cow crunching with depress'd head surpasses
      any statue,
And a mouse is miracle enough to stagger sextillions
      of infidels,
And I could come every afternoon of my life to look at the
      farmer's girl boiling her iron tea-kettle and baking
      short-cake.

I find I incorporate gneiss, coal, long-threaded moss, fruits,
      grains, esculent roots,
And am stucco'd with quadrupeds and birds all over,
And have distanced what is behind me for good reasons,
And call anything close again, when I desire it.

In vain the speeding or shyness;
In vain the plutonic rocks send their old heat against
      my approach;
In vain the mastodon retreats beneath its own powder'd bones;
In vain objects stand leagues off, and assume manifold shapes;
In vain the ocean settling in hollows, and the great monsters
      lying low;
In vain the buzzard houses herself with the sky;
In vain the snake slides through the creepers and logs;
In vain the elk takes to the inner passes of the woods;
In vain the razor-bill'd auk sails far north to Labrador;
I follow quickly, I ascend to the nest in the fissure of the cliff.

32

I think I could turn and live with animals, they are so placid
        and self-contain'd;
I stand and look at them long and long.

They do not sweat and whine about their condition;
They do not lie awake in the dark and weep for their sins;
They do not make me sick discussing their duty to God;
Not one is dissatisfied—not one is demented with the mania of
        owning things;
Not one kneels to another, nor to his kind that lived
        thousands of years ago;
Not one is respectable or industrious over the whole earth.

So they show their relations to me, and I accept them;
They bring me tokens of myself—they evince them plainly in
        their possession.

I wonder where they get those tokens:
Did I pass that way huge times ago, and negligently drop them?
Myself moving forward then and now and forever,
Gathering and showing more always and with velocity,
Infinite and omnigenous, and the like of these among them;
Not too exclusive toward the reachers of my remembrancers;
Picking out here one that I love, and now go with him on
        brotherly terms.

A gigantic beauty of a stallion, fresh and responsive to
        my caresses,
Head high in the forehead, wide between the ears,
Limbs glossy and supple, tail dusting the ground,
Eyes full of sparkling wickedness—ears finely cut, flexibly moving.

His nostrils dilate, as my heels embrace him;
His well-built limbs tremble with pleasure, as we race around
      and return.

I but use you a moment, then I resign you, stallion;
Why do I need your paces, when I myself out-gallop them?
Even, as I stand or sit, passing faster than you.

33

O swift wind! O space and time! now I see it is true, what I
      guessed at;
What I guess'd when I loaf'd on the grass;
What I guess'd while I lay alone in my bed,
And again as I walk'd the beach under the paling stars
      of the morning.

My ties and ballasts leave me – I travel – I sail – my elbows rest
      in the sea-gaps;
I skirt the sierras – my palms cover continents;
I am afoot with my vision.

By the city's quadrangular houses – in log huts – camping
      with lumbermen;
Along the ruts of the turnpike – along the dry gulch and
      rivulet bed;
Weeding my onion-patch, or hoeing rows of carrots and
      parsnips – crossing savannas – trailing in forests;
Prospecting – gold-digging – girdling the trees of a
      new purchase;
Scorch'd ankle-deep by the hot sand – hauling my boat down
      the shallow river;

Where the panther walks to and fro on a limb overhead –
        where the buck turns furiously at the hunter;
Where the rattlesnake suns his flabby length on a rock – where
        the otter is feeding on fish;
Where the alligator in his tough pimples sleeps by the bayou;
Where the black bear is searching for roots or honey – where
        the beaver pats the mud with his paddle-shaped tail;
Over the growing sugar – over the yellow-flower'd cotton
        plant – over the rice in its low moist field;
Over the sharp-peak'd farm house, with its scallop'd scum and
        slender shoots from the gutters;
Over the western persimmon – over the long-leav'd corn – over
        the delicate blue-flower flax;
Over the white and brown buckwheat, a hummer and buzzer
        there with the rest;
Over the dusky green of the rye as it ripples and shades
        in the breeze;
Scaling mountains, pulling myself cautiously up, holding on by
        low scragged limbs;
Walking the path worn in the grass, and beat through the
        leaves of the brush;
Where the quail is whistling betwixt the woods and the
        wheat-lot;
Where the bat flies in the Seventh-month eve – where the great
        gold-bug drops through the dark;
Where flails keep time on the barn floor;
Where the brook puts out of the roots of the old tree and
        flows to the meadow;
Where cattle stand and shake away flies with the tremulous
        shuddering of their hides;

Where the cheese-cloth hangs in the kitchen – where andirons
        straddle the hearth-slab – where cobwebs fall in
        festoons from the rafters;
Where trip-hammers crash – where the press is whirling
        its cylinders;
Wherever the human heart beats with terrible throes under
        its ribs;
Where the pear-shaped balloon is floating aloft, (floating in it
        myself, and looking composedly down;)
Where the life-car is drawn on the slip-noose – where the heat
        hatches pale-green eggs in the dented sand;
Where the she-whale swims with her calf, and never
        forsakes it;
Where the steam-ship trails hind-ways its long pennant
        of smoke;
Where the fin of the shark cuts like a black chip out of
        the water;
Where the half-burn'd brig is riding on unknown currents,
Where shells grow to her slimy deck – where the dead are
        corrupting below;
Where the dense-starr'd flag is borne at the head of the
        regiments;
Approaching Manhattan, up by the long-stretching island;
Under Niagara, the cataract falling like a veil over my
        countenance;
Upon a door-step – upon the horse-block of hard
        wood outside;
Upon the race-course, or enjoying picnics or jigs, or a good
        game of base-ball;
At he-festivals, with blackguard jibes, ironical license, bull-
        dances, drinking, laughter;

At the cider-mill, tasting the sweets of the brown mash,
        sucking the juice through a straw;
At apple-peelings, wanting kisses for all the red fruit I find;
At musters, beach-parties, friendly bees, huskings,
        house-raisings:
Where the mocking-bird sounds his delicious gurgles, cackles,
        screams, weeps;
Where the hay-rick stands in the barn-yard—where the dry-
        stalks are scattered—where the brood-cow waits
        in the hovel;
Where the bull advances to do his masculine work—where the
        stud to the mare—where the cock is treading the hen;
Where the heifers browse—where geese nip their food with
        short jerks;
Where sun-down shadows lengthen over the limitless and
        lonesome prairie;
Where herds of buffalo make a crawling spread of the square
        miles far and near;
Where the humming-bird shimmers—where the neck of the
        long-lived swan is curving and winding;
Where the laughing gull scoots by the shore, where she laughs
        her near-human laugh;
Where bee-hives range on a gray bench in the garden, half hid
        by the high weeds;
Where band-neck'd partridges roost in a ring on the ground
        with their heads out;
Where burial coaches enter the arch'd gates of a cemetery;
Where winter wolves bark amid wastes of snow and
        icicled trees;
Where the yellow-crown'd heron comes to the edge of the
        marsh at night and feeds upon small crabs;

Where the splash of swimmers and divers cools the
        warm noon;
Where the katy-did works her chromatic reed on the walnut-
        tree over the well;
Through patches of citrons and cucumbers with
        silver-wired leaves;
Through the salt-lick or orange glade, or under conical firs;
Through the gymnasium—through the curtain'd saloon—
        through the office or public hall;
Pleas'd with the native, and pleas'd with the foreign—pleas'd
        with the new and old;
Pleas'd with women, the homely as well as the handsome;
Pleas'd with the quakeress as she puts off her bonnet and
        talks melodiously;
Pleas'd with the tune of the choir of the white-wash'd church;
Pleas'd with the earnest words of the sweating Methodist
        preacher, or any preacher—impress'd seriously at the
        camp-meeting:
Looking in at the shop-windows of Broadway the whole
        forenoon— flatting the flesh of my nose on the thick
        plate-glass;
Wandering the same afternoon with my face turn'd up
        to the clouds,
My right and left arms round the sides of two friends, and I in
        the middle:
Coming home with the silent and dark-cheek'd bush-boy—
        (behind me he rides at the drape of the day;)
Far from the settlements, studying the print of animals' feet, or
        the moccasin print;
By the cot in the hospital, reaching lemonade to a
        feverish patient;

Nigh the coffin'd corpse when all is still, examining with
      a candle:
Voyaging to every port, to dicker and adventure;
Hurrying with the modern crowd, as eager and fickle as any;
Hot toward one I hate, ready in my madness to knife him;
Solitary at midnight in my back yard, my thoughts gone from
      me a long while;
Walking the old hills of Judea, with the beautiful gentle God
      by my side;
Speeding through space – speeding through heaven and
      the stars;
Speeding amid the seven satellites, and the broad ring, and the
      diameter of eighty thousand miles;
Speeding with tail'd meteors – throwing fire-balls like the rest;
Carrying the crescent child that carries its own full mother in
      its belly;
Storming, enjoying, planning, loving, cautioning,
Backing and filling, appearing and disappearing;
I tread day and night such roads.

I visit the orchards of spheres, and look at the product:
And look at quintillions ripen'd, and look at quintillions green.

I fly the flight of the fluid and swallowing soul;
My course runs below the soundings of plummets.

I help myself to material and immaterial;
No guard can shut me off, nor law prevent me.

I anchor my ship for a little while only;
My messengers continually cruise away, or bring their returns
      to me.

I go hunting polar furs and the seal—leaping chasms with a
        pike-pointed staff—clinging to topples of brittle
        and blue.

I ascend to the foretruck;
I take my place late at night in the crow's-nest;
We sail the arctic sea—it is plenty light enough;
Through the clear atmosphere I stretch around on the
        wonderful beauty;
The enormous masses of ice pass me, and I pass them—the
        scenery is plain in all directions;
The white-topt mountains show in the distance—I fling out my
        fancies toward them;
(We are approaching some great battle-field in which we are
        soon to be engaged;
We pass the colossal outposts of the encampment—we pass
        with still feet and caution;
Or we are entering by the suburbs some vast and ruin'd city;
The blocks and fallen architecture more than all the living
        cities of the globe.)

I am a free companion—I bivouac by invading watchfires.

I turn the bridegroom out of bed, and stay with the
        bride myself;
I tighten her all night to my thighs and lips.

My voice is the wife's voice, the screech by the rail
        of the stairs;
They fetch my man's body up, dripping and drown'd.

I understand the large hearts of heroes,

The courage of present times and all times;

How the skipper saw the crowded and rudderless wreck
of the steam-ship, and Death chasing it up and down
the storm;

How he knuckled tight, and gave not back one inch, and was
faithful of days and faithful of nights,

And chalk'd in large letters, on a board, *Be of good cheer, we
will not desert you:*

How he follow'd with them, and tack'd with them – and would
not give it up;

How he saved the drifting company at last:

How the lank loose-gown'd women look'd when boated from
the side of their prepared graves;

How the silent old-faced infants, and the lifted sick, and the
sharp-lipp'd unshaved men:

All this I swallow – it tastes good – I like it well – it
becomes mine;

I am the man – I suffer'd – I was there.

The disdain and calmness of olden martyrs;

The mother, condemn'd for a witch, burnt with dry wood, her
children gazing on;

The hounded slave that flags in the race, leans by the fence,
blowing, cover'd with sweat;

The twinges that sting like needles his legs and neck – the
murderous buckshot and the bullets;

All these I feel, or am.

I am the hounded slave, I wince at the bite of the dogs,

Hell and despair are upon me, crack and again crack
     the marksmen;
I clutch the rails of the fence, my gore dribs, thinn'd with the
     ooze of my skin;
I fall on the weeds and stones;
The riders spur their unwilling horses, haul close,
Taunt my dizzy ears, and beat me violently over the head with
     whip-stocks.

Agonies are one of my changes of garments;
I do not ask the wounded person how he feels – I myself
     become the wounded person;
My hurts turn livid upon me as I lean on a cane and observe.

I am the mash'd fireman with breast-bone broken;
Tumbling walls buried me in their debris;
Heat and smoke I inspired – I heard the yelling shouts
     of my comrades;
I heard the distant click of their picks and shovels;
They have clear'd the beams away – they tenderly lift me forth.

I lie in the night air in my red shirt – the pervading hush is for
     my sake;
Painless after all I lie, exhausted but not so unhappy;
White and beautiful are the faces around me – the heads are
     bared of their fire-caps;
The kneeling crowd fades with the light of the torches.

Distant and dead resuscitate;
They show as the dial or move as the hands of me – I am the
     clock myself.

I am an old artillerist—I tell of my fort's bombardment;
I am there again.

Again the long roll of the drummers,
Again the attacking cannon, mortars;
Again, to my listening ears, the cannon responsive.

I take part—I see and hear the whole;
The cries, curses, roar—the plaudits for well-aim'd shots;
The ambulanza slowly passing, trailing its red drip;
Workmen searching after damages, making indispensable
        repairs;
The fall of grenades through the rent roof—the fan-shaped
        explosion;
The whizz of limbs, heads, stone, wood, iron, high in the air.

Again gurgles the mouth of my dying general—he furiously
        waves with his hand;
He gasps through the clot, *Mind not me—mind—
        the entrenchments.*

34

Now I tell what I knew in Texas in my early youth;
(I tell not the fall of Alamo,
Not one escaped to tell the fall of Alamo,
The hundred and fifty are dumb yet at Alamo;)
'Tis the tale of the murder in cold blood of four hundred and
        twelve young men.

Retreating, they had form'd in a hollow square, with their
        baggage for breastworks;

Nine hundred lives out of the surrounding enemy's, nine times
        their number, was the price they took in advance;
Their colonel was wounded and their ammunition gone;
They treated for an honorable capitulation, receiv'd writing
        and seal, gave up their arms, and march'd back
        prisoners of war.

They were the glory of the race of rangers;
Matchless with horse, rifle, song, supper, courtship,
Large, turbulent, generous, handsome, proud, and affectionate,
Bearded, sunburnt, drest in the free costume of hunters,
Not a single one over thirty years of age.

The second First-day morning they were brought out in
        squads, and massacred – it was beautiful early summer;
The work commenced about five o'clock, and was over
        by eight.

None obey'd the command to kneel;
Some made a mad and helpless rush – some stood stark
        and straight;
A few fell at once, shot in the temple or heart – the living and
        dead lay together;
The maim'd and mangled dug in the dirt – the newcomers saw
        them there;
Some, half-kill'd, attempted to crawl away;
These were despatch'd with bayonets, or batter'd with the
        blunts of muskets;
A youth not seventeen years old seiz'd his assassin till two
        more came to release him;
The three were all torn, and cover'd with the boy's blood.

At eleven o'clock began the burning of the bodies:
That is the tale of the murder of the four hundred and twelve
    young men.

35

Would you hear of an old-fashion'd sea-fight?
Would you learn who won by the light of the moon and stars?
List to the story as my grandmother's father, the sailor, told it
    to me.

Our foe was no skulk in his ship, I tell you, (said he;)
He was the surly English pluck—and there is no tougher or
    truer, and never was, and never will be;
Along the lower'd eve he came, horribly raking us.

We closed with him—the yards entangled—the cannon touch'd;
My captain lash'd fast with his own hands.

We had receiv'd some eighteen pound shots under the water;
On our lower-gun-deck two large pieces had burst at the first
    fire, killing all around, and blowing up overhead.

Fighting at sun-down, fighting at dark;
Ten o'clock at night, the full moon well up, our leaks on the
    gain, and five feet of water reported;
The master-at-arms loosing the prisoners confined in the
    afterhold, to give them a chance for themselves.

The transit to and from the magazine is now stopt by
    the sentinels,
They see so many strange faces, they do not know whom
    to trust.

Our frigate takes fire;
The other asks if we demand quarter?
If our colors are struck, and the fighting is done?

Now I laugh content, for I hear the voice of my little captain,
We have not struck, he composedly cries, *we have just begun our
        part of the fighting.*

Only three guns are in use;
One is directed by the captain himself against the enemy's
        mainmast;
Two, well served with grape and canister, silence his musketry
        and clear his decks.

The tops alone second the fire of this little battery, especially
        the main-top;
They hold out bravely during the whole of the action.

Not a moment's cease;
The leaks gain fast on the pumps—the fire eats toward the
        powder-magazine.

One of the pumps has been shot away—it is generally thought
        we are sinking.

Serene stands the little captain;
He is not hurried—his voice is neither high nor low;
His eyes give more light to us than our battle-lanterns.

Toward twelve at night, there in the beams of the moon, they
        surrender to us.

36

Stretch'd and still lies the midnight;
Two great hulls motionless on the breast of the darkness;
Our vessel riddled and slowly sinking—preparations to pass to
       the one we have conquer'd;
The captain on the quarter-deck coldly giving his orders
       through a countenance white as a sheet;
Near by, the corpse of the child that serv'd in the cabin;
The dead face of an old salt with long white hair and carefully
       curl'd whiskers;
The flames, spite of all that can be done, flickering aloft
       and below;
The husky voices of the two or three officers yet fit for duty;
Formless stacks of bodies, and bodies by themselves—dabs of
       flesh upon the masts and spars,
Cut of cordage, dangle of rigging, slight shock of the soothe
       of waves,
Black and impassive guns, litter of powder-parcels,
       strong scent,
Delicate sniffs of sea-breeze, smells of sedgy grass and fields by
       the shore, death-messages given in charge to survivors,
The hiss of the surgeon's knife, the gnawing teeth of his saw,
Wheeze, cluck, swash of falling blood, short wild scream, and
       long, dull tapering groan;
These so—these irretrievable.

37

O Christ! This is mastering me!
In at the conquer'd doors they crowd. I am possess'd.

I embody all presences outlaw'd or suffering;
See myself in prison shaped like another man,
And feel the dull unintermitted pain.

For me the keepers of convicts shoulder their carbines and
        keep watch;
It is I let out in the morning, and barr'd at night.

Not a mutineer walks handcuff'd to jail, but I am handcuff'd to
        him and walk by his side;
(I am less the jolly one there, and more the silent one, with
        sweat on my twitching lips.)

Not a youngster is taken for larceny, but I go up too, and am
        tried and sentenced.

Not a cholera patient lies at the last gasp, but I also lie at the
        last gasp;
My face is ash-color'd—my sinews gnarl—away from me
        people retreat.

Askers embody themselves in me, and I am embodied
        in them;
I project my hat, sit shame-faced, and beg.

38

Enough! enough! enough!
Somehow I have been stunn'd. Stand back!
Give me a little time beyond my cuff'd head, slumbers,
        dreams, gaping;
I discover myself on the verge of a usual mistake.

That I could forget the mockers and insults!
That I could forget the trickling tears, and the blows of the
        bludgeons and hammers!
That I could look with a separate look on my own crucifixion
        and bloody crowning.

I remember now;
I resume the overstaid fraction;
The grave of rock multiplies what has been confided to it, or
        to any graves;
Corpses rise, gashes heal, fastenings roll from me.

I troop forth replenish'd with supreme power, one of an
        average unending procession;
Inland and sea-coast we go, and we pass all boundary lines;
Our swift ordinances on their way over the whole earth;
The blossoms we wear in our hats the growth of thousands
        of years.

Eleves, I salute you! come forward!
Continue your annotations, continue your questionings.

39

The friendly and flowing savage, Who is he?
Is he waiting for civilization, or past it, and mastering it?

Is he some south-westerner, rais'd out-doors? Is he Kanadian?
Is he from the Mississippi country? Iowa, Oregon, California?
        the mountains? prairie-life, bush-life? or from the sea?

Wherever he goes, men and women accept and desire him;
They desire he should like them, touch them, speak to them,
        stay with them.

Behavior lawless as snow-flakes, words simple as grass,
        uncomb'd head, laughter, and naiveté,
Slow-stepping feet, common features, common modes
        and emanations;
They descend in new forms from the tips of his fingers;
They are wafted with the odor of his body or breath – they fly
        out of the glance of his eyes.

40

Flaunt of the sunshine, I need not your bask, – lie over!
You light surfaces only – I force surfaces and depths also.

Earth! you seem to look for something at my hands;
Say, old Top-knot! what do you want?

Man or woman! I might tell how I like you,
        but cannot;
And might tell what it is in me, and what it is in you, but
        cannot;
And might tell that pining I have – that pulse of my nights
        and days.

Behold! I do not give lectures, or a little charity;
When I give, I give myself.

You there, impotent, loose in the knees!
Open your scarf'd chops till I blow grit within you;
Spread your palms, and lift the flaps of your pockets;

I am not to be denied—I compel—I have stores plenty
        and to spare;
And anything I have I bestow.

I do not ask who you are—that is not so important to me;
You can do nothing, and be nothing, but what I will
        infold you.

To cotton-field drudge or cleaner of privies I lean;
On his right cheek I put the family kiss,
And in my soul I swear, I never will deny him.

On women fit for conception I start bigger and nimbler babes;
(This day I am jetting the stuff of far more arrogant republics.)

To any one dying—thither I speed, and twist the knob of
        the door;
Turn the bed-clothes toward the foot of the bed;
Let the physician and the priest go home.

I seize the descending man, and raise him with resistless will.

O despairer, here is my neck;
By God! you shall not go down! Hang your whole weight
        upon me.

I dilate you with tremendous breath—I buoy you up;
Every room of the house do I fill with an arm'd force,
Lovers of me, bafflers of graves.

Sleep! I and they keep guard all night;
Not doubt—not decease shall dare to lay finger upon you;

I have embraced you, and henceforth possess you to myself;
And when you rise in the morning you will find what I tell
      you is so.

41

I am he bringing help for the sick as they pant on their backs;
And for strong upright men I bring yet more needed help.

I heard what was said of the universe;
Heard it and heard it of several thousand years:
It is middling well as far as it goes,—But is that all?

Magnifying and applying come I,
Outbidding at the start the old cautious hucksters,
Taking myself the exact dimensions of Jehovah,
Lithographing Kronos, Zeus his son, and Hercules
      his grandson;
Buying drafts of Osiris, Isis, Belus, Brahma, Buddha,
In my portfolio placing Manito loose, Allah on a leaf, the
      crucifix engraved,
With Odin and the hideous-faced Mexitli, and every idol
      and image;
Taking them all for what they are worth, and not a cent more;
Admitting they were alive and did the work of their days;
(They bore mites, as for unfledg'd birds, who have now to rise
      and fly and sing for themselves;)
Accepting the rough deific sketches to fill out better in
      myself— bestowing them freely on each man and
      woman I see;
Discovering as much, or more, in a framer framing a house;
Putting higher claims for him there with his roll'd-up sleeves,
      driving the mallet and chisel;

Not objecting to special revelations—considering a curl of
        smoke, or a hair on the back of my hand, just as
        curious as any revelation;
Lads ahold of fire-engines and hook-and-ladder ropes no less
        to me than the Gods of the antique wars;
Minding their voices peal through the crash of destruction,
Their brawny limbs passing safe over charr'd laths—their white
        foreheads whole and unhurt out of the flames:
By the mechanic's wife with her babe at her nipple interceding
        for every person born;
Three scythes at harvest whizzing in a row from three lusty
        angels with shirts bagg'd out at their waists;
The snag-tooth'd hostler with red hair redeeming sins past and
        to come,
Selling all he possesses, traveling on foot to fee lawyers for his
        brother, and sit by him while he is tried for forgery;
What was strewn in the amplest strewing the square rod about
        me, and not filling the square rod then;
The bull and the bug never worship'd half enough;
Dung and dirt more admirable than was dream'd;
The supernatural of no account—myself waiting my time to be
        one of the Supremes;
The day getting ready for me when I shall do as much good as
        the best, and be as prodigious:
By my life lumps! becoming already a creator;
Putting myself here and now to the ambush'd womb
        of the shadows.

42

A call in the midst of the crowd;
My own voice, orotund, sweeping, and final.

Come my children;
Come my boys and girls, my women, household,
        and intimates;
Now the performer launches his nerve—he has pass'd his
        prelude on the reeds within.

Easily written, loose-finger'd chords! I feel the thrum of your
        climax and close.

My head slues round on my neck;
Music rolls, but not from the organ;
Folks are around me, but they are no household of mine.

Ever the hard, unsunk ground;
Ever the eaters and drinkers—ever the upward and downward
        sun—ever the air and the ceaseless tides;
Ever myself and my neighbors, refreshing, wicked, real;
Ever the old inexplicable query—ever that thorn'd thumb—that
        breath of itches and thirsts;
Ever the vexer's *hoot! hoot!* till we find where the sly one hides,
        and bring him forth;
Ever love—ever the sobbing liquid of life;
Ever the bandage under the chin—ever the tressels of death.

Here and there, with dimes on the eyes, walking;
To feed the greed of the belly, the brains liberally spooning;
Tickets buying, taking, selling, but in to the feast never
        once going;
Many sweating, ploughing, thrashing, and then the chaff for
        payment receiving;
A few idly owning, and they the wheat continually claiming.

This is the city, and I am one of the citizens;
Whatever interests the rest interests me – politics, wars,
        markets, newspapers, schools,
Benevolent societies, improvements, banks, tariffs, steamships,
        factories, stocks, stores, real estate, and personal estate.

The little plentiful mannikins, skipping around in collars and
        tail'd coats,
I am aware who they are – (they are positively not worms
        or fleas.)

I acknowledge the duplicates of myself – the weakest and
        shallowest is deathless with me;
What I do and say, the same waits for them;
Every thought that flounders in me, the same flounders
        in them.

I know perfectly well my own egotism;
I know my omnivorous lines, and will not write any less;
And would fetch you, whoever you are, flush with myself.

No words of routine are mine,
But abruptly to question, to leap beyond, yet nearer bring:
This printed and bound book – but the printer, and the
        printing-office boy?
The well-taken photographs – but your wife or friend close and
        solid in your arms?
The black ship, mail'd with iron, her mighty guns in her
        turrets – but the pluck of the captain and engineers?
In the houses, the dishes and fare and furniture – but the host
        and hostess, and the look out of their eyes?

The sky up there—yet here, or next door, or across the way?
The saints and sages in history—but you yourself?
Sermons, creeds, theology—but the fathomless human brain,
And what is reason? and what is love? and what is life?

43

I do not despise you, priests;
My faith is the greatest of faiths, and the least of faiths,
Enclosing worship ancient and modern, and all between
        ancient and modern,
Believing I shall come again upon the earth after five
        thousand years,
Waiting responses from oracles, honoring the Gods, saluting
        the sun,
Making a fetish of the first rock or stump, powwowing with
        sticks in the circle of obis,
Helping the lama or brahmin as he trims the lamps
        of the idols,
Dancing yet through the streets in a phallic procession—rapt
        and austere in the woods, a gymnosophist,
Drinking mead from the skull-cup—to Shastas and Vedas
        admirant—minding the Koran,
Walking the teokallis, spotted with gore from the stone and
        knife, beating the serpent-skin drum,
Accepting the Gospels—accepting him that was crucified,
        knowing assuredly that he is divine,
To the mass kneeling, or the puritan's prayer rising, or sitting
        patiently in a pew,
Ranting and frothing in my insane crisis, or waiting dead-like
        till my spirit arouses me,

Looking forth on pavement and land, or outside of pavement
        and land,
Belonging to the winders of the circuit of circuits.

One of that centripetal and centrifugal gang, I turn and talk,
        like a man leaving charges before a journey.

Down-hearted doubters, dull and excluded,
Frivolous, sullen, moping, angry, affected, dishearten'd,
        atheistical;
I know every one of you—I know the sea of torment, doubt,
        despair and unbelief.

How the flukes splash!
How they contort, rapid as lightning, with spasms, and spouts
        of blood!

Be at peace, bloody flukes of doubters and sullen mopers;
I take my place among you as much as among any;
The past is the push of you, me, all, precisely the same,
And what is yet untried and afterward is for you, me, all,
        precisely the same.

I do not know what is untried and afterward;
But I know it will in its turn prove sufficient, and cannot fail.

Each who passes is consider'd—each who stops is consider'd—
        not a single one can it fail.

It cannot fail the young man who died and was buried,
Nor the young woman who died and was put by his side,

Nor the little child that peep'd in at the door, and then drew
       back, and was never seen again,
Nor the old man who has lived without purpose, and feels it
       with bitterness worse than gall.
Nor him in the poor house, tubercled by rum and the
       bad disorder,
Nor the numberless slaughter'd and wreck'd – nor the brutish
       koboo call'd the ordure of humanity,
Nor the sacks merely floating with open mouths for food to
       slip in,
Nor anything in the earth, or down in the oldest graves
       of the earth,
Nor anything in the myriads of spheres – nor one of the
       myriads of myriads that inhabit them,
Nor the present – nor the least wisp that is known.

44

It is time to explain myself – Let us stand up.

What is known I strip away;
I launch all men and women forward with me into
       THE UNKNOWN.

The clock indicates the moment – but what does eternity
       indicate?

We have thus far exhausted trillions of winters and summers;
There are trillions ahead, and trillions ahead of them.

Births have brought us richness and variety,
And other births will bring us richness and variety.

I do not call one greater and one smaller;
That which fills its period and place is equal to any.

Were mankind murderous or jealous upon you, my brother,
        my sister?
I am sorry for you–they are not murderous or jealous
        upon me;
All has been gentle with me–I keep no account with
        lamentation;
(What have I to do with lamentation?)

I am an acme of things accomplish'd, and I an encloser of
        things to be.

My feet strike an apex of the apices of the stairs;
On every step bunches of ages, and larger bunches between
        the steps;
All below duly travel'd, and still I mount and mount.

Rise after rise bow the phantoms behind me;
Afar down I see the huge first Nothing–I know I was
        even there;
I waited unseen and always, and slept through the
        lethargic mist,
And took my time, and took no hurt from the fetid carbon.

Long I was hugg'd close–long and long.

Immense have been the preparations for me,
Faithful and friendly the arms that have help'd me.

Cycles ferried my cradle, rowing and rowing like
          cheerful boatmen;
For room to me stars kept aside in their own rings;
They sent influences to look after what was to hold me.

Before I was born out of my mother, generations guided me;
My embryo has never been torpid – nothing could overlay it.

For it the nebula cohered to an orb,
The long slow strata piled to rest it on,
Vast vegetables gave it sustenance,
Monstrous sauroids transported it in their mouths, and
          deposited it with care.

All forces have been steadily employ'd to complete and
          delight me;
Now on this spot I stand with my robust Soul.

45

O span of youth! Ever-push'd elasticity!
O manhood, balanced, florid, and full.

My lovers suffocate me!
Crowding my lips, thick in the pores of my skin,
Jostling me through streets and public halls – coming naked to
          me at night,
Crying by day *Ahoy!* from the rocks of the river – swinging and
          chirping over my head,
Calling my name from flower-beds, vines, tangled underbrush,
Lighting on every moment of my life,
Bussing my body with soft balsamic busses,

Noiselessly passing handfuls out of their hearts, and giving
    them to be mine.

Old age superbly rising! O welcome, ineffable grace of
    dying days!

Every condition promulges not only itself–it promulges what
    grows after and out of itself,
And the dark hush promulges as much as any.

I open my scuttle at night and see the far-sprinkled systems,
And all I see, multiplied as high as I can cipher, edge but the
    rim of the farther systems.

Wider and wider they spread, expanding, always expanding,
Outward and outward, and forever outward.

My sun has his sun, and round him obediently wheels,
He joins with his partners a group of superior circuit,
And greater sets follow, making specks of the greatest
    inside them.

There is no stoppage, and never can be stoppage;
If I, you, and the worlds, and all beneath or upon their
    surfaces, were this moment reduced back to a pallid
    float, it would not avail in the long run;
We should surely bring up again where we now stand,
And as surely go as much farther–and then farther and farther.

A few quadrillions of eras, a few octillions of cubic leagues, do
    not hazard the span, or make it impatient;
They are but parts–anything is but a part.

See ever so far, there is limitless space outside of that;
Count ever so much, there is limitless time around that.

My rendezvous is appointed – it is certain;
The Lord will be there, and wait till I come, on perfect terms;
(The great Camerado, the lover true for whom I pine,
          will be there.)

46

I know I have the best of time and space, and was never
          measured, and never will be measured.

I tramp a perpetual journey – (come listen all!)
My signs are a rain-proof coat, good shoes, and a staff cut from
          the woods;
No friend of mine takes his ease in my chair;
I have no chair, no church, no philosophy;
I lead no man to a dinner-table, library, or exchange;
But each man and each woman of you I lead upon a knoll,
My left hand hooking you round the waist,
My right hand pointing to landscapes of continents, and a
          plain public road.

Not I – not any one else, can travel that road for you,
You must travel it for yourself.

It is not far – it is within reach;
Perhaps you have been on it since you were born, and did not
          know;
Perhaps it is every where on water and on land.

Shoulder your duds, dear son, and I will mine, and let us
     hasten forth,
Wonderful cities and free nations we shall fetch as we go.

If you tire, give me both burdens, and rest the chuff of your
     hand on my hip,
And in due time you shall repay the same service to me;
For after we start, we never lie by again.

This day before dawn I ascended a hill, and look'd at the
     crowded heaven,
And I said to my Spirit, *When we become the enfolders of those
     orbs, and the pleasure and knowledge of everything in
     them, shall we be fill'd and satisfied then?*
And my Spirit said, *No, we but level that lift, to pass and
     continue beyond.*

You are also asking me questions, and I hear you;
I answer that I cannot answer—you must find out for yourself.

Sit a while, dear son;
Here are biscuits to eat, and here is milk to drink;
But as soon as you sleep, and renew yourself in sweet clothes, I
     kiss you with a good-bye kiss, and open the gate for
     your egress hence.

Long enough have you dream'd contemptible dreams;
Now I wash the gum from your eyes;
You must habit yourself to the dazzle of the light, and of every
     moment of your life.

Long have you timidly waded, holding a plank by the shore;
Now I will you to be a bold swimmer,

To jump off in the midst of the sea, rise again, nod to me,
      shout, and laughingly dash with your hair.

47

I am the teacher of athletes;
He that by me spreads a wider breast than my own, proves
      the width of my own;
He most honors my style who learns under it to destroy
      the teacher.

The boy I love, the same becomes a man, not through derived
      power, but in his own right,
Wicked, rather than virtuous out of conformity or fear,
Fond of his sweetheart, relishing well his steak,
Unrequited love, or a slight, cutting him worse than sharp
      steel cuts,
First-rate to ride, to fight, to hit the bull's eye, to sail a skiff, to
      sing a song, or play on the banjo,
Preferring scars, and the beard, and faces pitted with small-
      pox, over all latherers,
And those well tann'd to those that keep out of the sun.

I teach straying from me—yet who can stray from me?
I follow you, whoever you are, from the present hour;
My words itch at your ears till you understand them.

I do not say these things for a dollar, or to fill up the time
      while I wait for a boat;
It is you talking just as much as myself—I act as the tongue of you;
Tied in your mouth, in mine it begins to be loosen'd.

I swear I will never again mention love or death inside
      a house,

And I swear I will never translate myself at all, only to him or
    her who privately stays with me in the open air.

If you would understand me, go to the heights or water shore;
The nearest gnat is an explanation, and a drop or motion of
    waves a key;
The maul, the oar, the hand-saw, second my words.

No shutter'd room or school can commune with me,
But roughs and little children better than they.

The young mechanic is closest to me—he knows me well;
The woodman, that takes his axe and jug with him, shall take
    me with him all day;
The farm-boy, ploughing in the field, feels good at the sound
    of my voice;
In vessels that sail, my words sail—I go with fishermen and
    seamen, and love them.

The soldier camp'd, or upon the march, is mine;
On the night ere the pending battle, many seek me, and I do
    not fail them
On the solemn night (it may be their last,) those that know
    me, seek me.

My face rubs to the hunter's face, when he lies down alone in
    his blanket;
The driver, thinking of me, does not mind the jolt of
    his wagon;
The young mother and old mother comprehend me;

The girl and the wife rest the needle a moment, and forget
      where they are;
They and all would resume what I have told them.

48

I have said that the soul is not more than the body,
And I have said that the body is not more than the soul;
And nothing, not God, is greater to one than one's self is,
And whoever walks a furlong without sympathy, walks to his
      own funeral, drest in his shroud,
And I or you, pocketless of a dime, may purchase the pick of
      the earth,
And to glance with an eye, or show a bean in its pod,
      confounds the learning of all times,
And there is no trade or employment but the young man
      following it may become a hero,
And there is no object so soft but it makes a hub for the
      wheel'd universe,
And I say to any man or woman, Let your soul stand cool and
      composed before a million universes.

And I say to mankind, Be not curious about God,
For I, who am curious about each, am not curious about God
(No array of terms can say how much I am at peace about
      God, and about death.)

I hear and behold God in every object, yet understand God not
      in the least,
Nor do I understand who there can be more wonderful
      than myself.

Why should I wish to see God better than this day?
I see something of God each hour of the twenty-four, and each
      moment then;
In the faces of men and women I see God, and in my own face
      in the glass;
I find letters from God dropt in the street—and every one is
      sign'd by God's name,
And I leave them where they are, for I know that wheresoe'er
      I go,
Others will punctually come forever and ever.

49

And as to you Death, and you bitter hug of mortality, it is idle
      to try to alarm me.

To his work without flinching the accoucheur comes;
I see the elder-hand, pressing, receiving, supporting;
I recline by the sills of the exquisite flexible doors,
And mark the outlet, and mark the relief and escape.

And as to you, Corpse, I think you are good manure—but that
      does not offend me;
I smell the white roses sweet-scented and growing,
I reach to the leafy lips—I reach to the polish'd breasts
      of melons.

And as to you Life, I reckon you are the leavings of
      many deaths;
(No doubt I have died myself ten thousand times before.)

I hear you whispering there, O stars of heaven;
O suns! O grass of graves! O perpetual transfers
        and promotions!
If you do not say anything, how can I say anything?

Of the turbid pool that lies in the autumn forest,
Of the moon that descends the steeps of the soughing twilight,
Toss, sparkles of day and dusk! toss on the black stems that
        decay in the muck!
Toss to the moaning gibberish of the dry limbs.

I ascend from the moon, I ascend from the night;
I perceive that the ghastly glimmer is noonday sunbeams
        reflected;
And debouch to the steady and central from the offspring
        great or small.

50

There is that in me — I do not know what it is — but I know it is
        in me.

Wrench'd and sweaty — calm and cool then my body becomes;
I sleep — I sleep long.

I do not know it — it is without name — it is a word unsaid;
It is not in any dictionary, utterance, symbol.

Something it swings on more than the earth I swing on;
To it the creation is the friend whose embracing awakes me.

Perhaps I might tell more. Outlines! I plead for my brothers
        and sisters.

Do you see, O my brothers and sisters?
It is not chaos or death—it is form, union, plan—it is eternal
     life—it is HAPPINESS.

51

The mast and present wilt—I have fill'd them, emptied them,
And proceed to fill my next fold of the future.

Listener up there! Here, you! What have you to confide to me?
Look in my face, while I snuff the sidle of evening;
Talk honestly—no one else hears you, and I stay only a
     minute longer.

Do I contradict myself?
Very well, then, I contradict myself;
(I am large—I contain multitudes.)

I concentrate toward them that are nigh—I wait on the
     door-slab.

Who has done his day's work? Who will soonest be through
     with his supper?
Who wishes to walk with me?

Will you speak before I am gone? Will you prove already
     too late?

52

The spotted hawk swoops by and accuses me—he complains of
     my gab and my loitering.

I too am not a bit tamed—I too am untranslatable;
I sound my barbaric yawp over the roofs of the world.

The last scud of day holds back for me;
It flings my likeness after the rest, and true as any, on the
        shadow'd wilds;
It coaxes me to the vapor and the dusk.

I depart as air—I shake my white locks at the runaway sun;
I effuse my flesh in eddies, and drift it in lacy jags.

I bequeathe myself to the dirt, to grow from the grass I love;
If you want me again, look for me under your boot-soles.

You will hardly know who I am, or what I mean;
But I shall be good health to you nevertheless,
And filter and fiber your blood.

Failing to fetch me at first, keep encouraged;
Missing me one place, search another;
I stop some where, waiting for you.

From Pent-up Aching Rivers

First published in 1860

From pent-up, aching rivers;
From that of myself, without which I were nothing;
From what I am determin'd to make illustrious, even if I stand
        sole among men;

From my own voice resonant – singing the phallus,
Singing the song of procreation,
Singing the need of superb children, and therein superb
      grown people,
Singing the muscular urge and the blending,
Singing the bedfellow's song, (O resistless yearning!
O for any and each, the body correlative attracting!
O for you, whoever you are, your correlative body! O it, more
      than all else, you delighting!)
– From the hungry gnaw that eats me night and day;
From native moments – from bashful pains – singing them;
Singing something yet unfound, though I have diligently
      sought it, many a long year;
Singing the true song of the Soul, fitful, at random;
Singing what, to the Soul, entirely redeem'd her, the faithful
      one, even the prostitute, who detain'd me when I went
      to the city;
Singing the song of prostitutes;
Renascent with grossest Nature, or among animals;
Of that – of them, and what goes with them, my poems
      informing;
Of the smell of apples and lemons – of the pairing of birds,
Of the wet of woods – of the lapping of waves,
Of the mad pushes of waves upon the land – I them chanting;
The overture lightly sounding – the strain anticipating;
The welcome nearness – the sight of the perfect body;
The swimmer swimming naked in the bath, or motionless on
      his back lying and floating;
The female form approaching – I, pensive, love-flesh
      tremulous, aching;
The divine list, for myself or you, or for any one, making;

The face – the limbs – the index from head to foot, and what it
     arouses;
The mystic deliria – the madness amorous – the utter
     abandonment;
(Hark close, and still, what I now whisper to you,
I love you – O you entirely possess me,
O I wish that you and I escape from the rest, and go utterly
     off – O free and lawless,
Two hawks in the air – two fishes swimming in the sea not
     more lawless than we;)
–The furious storm through me careering – I passionately
     trembling;
The oath of the inseparableness of two together – of the woman
     that loves me, and whom I love more than my life –
     that oath swearing;
(O I willingly stake all, for you!
O let me be lost, if it must be so!
O you and I – what is it to us what the rest do or think?
What is all else to us? only that we enjoy each other, and
     exhaust each other, if it must be so:)
–From the master – the pilot I yield the vessel to;
The general commanding me, commanding all – from him
     permission taking;
From time the programme hastening, (I have loiter'd too long,
     as it is;)
From sex – From the warp and from the woof;
(To talk to the perfect girl who understands me,
To waft to her these from my own lips – to effuse them from
     my own body;)
From privacy – from frequent repinings alone;
From plenty of persons near, and yet the right person
     not near;

From the soft sliding of hands over me, and thrusting of
        fingers through my hair and beard;
From the long sustain'd kiss upon the mouth or bosom;
From the close pressure that makes me or any man drunk,
        fainting with excess;
From what the divine husband knows—from the work of
        fatherhood;
From exultation, victory, and relief—from the bedfellow's
        embrace in the night;
From the act-poems of eyes, hands, hips, and bosoms,
From the cling of the trembling arm,
From the bending curve and the clinch,
From side by side, the pliant coverlid off-throwing,
From the one so unwilling to have me leave—and me just as
        unwilling to leave,
(Yet a moment, O tender waiter, and I return;)
—From the hour of shining stars and dropping dews,
From the night, a moment, I, emerging, flitting out,
Celebrate you, act divine—and you, children prepared for,
And you, stalwart loins.

I SING THE BODY ELECTRIC

First published in 1855

1

I SING THE Body electric;
The armies of those I love engirth me, and I engirth them;
They will not let me off till I go with them, respond to them,
And discorrupt them, and charge them full with the charge
        of the Soul.

Was it doubted that those who corrupt their own bodies
      conceal themselves?
And if those who defile the living are as bad as they who
      defile the dead?
And if the body does not do as much as the Soul?
And if the body were not the Soul, what is the Soul?

2

The love of the Body of man or woman balks account—the
      body itself balks account;
That of the male is perfect, and that of the female is perfect.

The expression of the face balks account;
But the expression of a well-made man appears not only
      in his face;
It is in his limbs and joints also, it is curiously in the joints of
      his hips and wrists;
It is in his walk, the carriage of his neck, the flex of his waist
      and knees—dress does not hide him;
The strong, sweet, supple quality he has, strikes through the
      cotton and flannel;
To see him pass conveys as much as the best poem,
      perhaps more;
You linger to see his back, and the back of his neck and
      shoulder-side.

The sprawl and fulness of babes, the bosoms and heads of
      women, the folds of their dress, their style as we pass
      in the street, the contour of their shape downwards,

The swimmer naked in the swimming-bath, seen as he swims
        through the transparent green-shine, or lies with his
        face up, and rolls silently to and fro in the heave
        of the water,
The bending forward and backward of rowers in row-boats—
        the horseman in his saddle,
Girls, mothers, house-keepers, in all their performances,
The group of laborers seated at noon-time with their open
        dinner-kettles, and their wives waiting,
The female soothing a child—the farmer's daughter in the
        garden or cow-yard,
The young fellow hoeing corn—the sleigh-driver guiding his
        six horses through the crowd,
The wrestle of wrestlers, two apprentice-boys, quite grown,
        lusty, good-natured, native-born, out on the vacant lot
        at sundown, after work,
The coats and caps thrown down, the embrace of love
        and resistance,
The upper-hold and the under-hold, the hair rumpled over
        and blinding the eyes;
The march of firemen in their own costumes, the play of
        masculine muscle through clean-setting trowsers and
        waist-straps,
The slow return from the fire, the pause when the bell strikes
        suddenly again, and the listening on the alert,
The natural, perfect, varied attitudes—the bent head, the curv'd
        neck, and the counting;
Such-like I love—I loosen myself, pass freely, am at the
        mother's breast with the little child,
Swim with the swimmers, wrestle with wrestlers, march in line
        with the firemen, and pause, listen, and count.

3

I know a man, a common farmer – the father of five sons;
And in them were the fathers of sons – and in them were the
       fathers of sons.

This man was of wonderful vigor, calmness, beauty of person;
The shape of his head, the pale yellow and white of his hair
       and beard, and the immeasurable meaning of his black
       eyes – the richness and breadth of his manners,
These I used to go and visit him to see – he was wise also;
He was six feet tall, he was over eighty years old – his sons
       were massive, clean, bearded, tan-faced, handsome;
They and his daughters loved him – all who saw him
       loved him;
They did not love him by allowance – they loved him with
       personal love;
He drank water only – the blood show'd like scarlet through
       the clear-brown skin of his face;
He was a frequent gunner and fisher – he sail'd his boat
       himself – he had a fine one presented to him by a ship-
       joiner – he had fowling-pieces, presented to him by
       men that loved him;
When he went with his five sons and many grand-sons to
       hunt or fish, you would pick him out as the most
       beautiful and vigorous of the gang.

You would wish long and long to be with him – you would
       wish to sit by him in the boat, that you and he might
       touch each other.

4

I have perceiv'd that to be with those I like is enough,
To stop in company with the rest at evening is enough,
To be surrounded by beautiful, curious, breathing, laughing
          flesh is enough,
To pass among them, or touch any one, or rest my arm ever so
          lightly round his or her neck for a moment—what is
          this, then?
I do not ask any more delight—I swim in it, as in a sea.

There is something in staying close to men and women, and
          looking on them, and in the contact and odor of them,
          that pleases the soul well;
All things please the soul—but these the soul well.

5

This is the female form;
A divine nimbus exhales from it from head to foot;
It attracts with fierce undeniable attraction!
I am drawn by its breath as if I were no more than a helpless
          vapor—all falls aside but myself and it;
Books, art, religion, time, the visible and solid earth, the
          atmosphere and the clouds, and what was expected of
          heaven or fear'd of hell, are now consumed;
Mad filaments, ungovernable shoots play out of it—the
          response likewise ungovernable;
Hair, bosom, hips, bend of legs, negligent falling hands, all
          diffused—mine too diffused;
Ebb stung by the flow, and flow stung by the ebb—love-flesh
          swelling and deliciously aching;

Limitless limpid jets of love hot and enormous, quivering jelly
      of love, white-blow and delirious juice;
Bridegroom night of love, working surely and softly into the
      prostrate dawn;
Undulating into the willing and yielding day,
Lost in the cleave of the clasping and sweet-flesh'd day.

This is the nucleus—after the child is born of woman, the man
      is born of woman;
This the bath of birth—this is the merge of small and large,
      and the outlet again.

Be not ashamed, women—your privilege encloses the rest, and
      is the exit of the rest;
You are the gates of the body, and you are the gates of the soul.

The female contains all qualities, and tempers them—she is in
      her place, and moves with perfect balance;
She is all things duly veil'd—she is both passive and active;
She is to conceive daughters as well as sons, and sons as well
      as daughters.

As I see my soul reflected in nature;
As I see through a mist, one with inexpressible completeness
      and beauty,
See the bent head, and arms folded over the breast—the
      female I see.

6

The male is not less the soul, nor more—he too is in his place;
He too is all qualities—he is action and power;

The flush of the known universe is in him;
Scorn becomes him well, and appetite and defiance become
        him well;
The wildest largest passions, bliss that is utmost, sorrow that is
        utmost, become him well—pride is for him;
The full spread pride of man is calming and excellent to
        the soul;
Knowledge becomes him—he likes it always—he brings
        everything to the test of himself;
Whatever the survey, whatever the sea and the sail, he strikes
        soundings at last only here;
(Where else does he strike soundings, except here?)

The man's body is sacred, and the woman's body is sacred;
No matter who it is, it is sacred;
Is it a slave? Is it one of the dull-faced immigrants just landed
        on the wharf?
Each belongs here or anywhere, just as much as the well-off—
        just as much as you;
Each has his or her place in the procession.

(All is a procession;
The universe is a procession, with measured and
        beautiful motion.)

Do you know so much yourself, that you call the slave or the
        dull-face ignorant?
Do you suppose you have a right to a good sight, and he or
        she has no right to a sight?

Do you think matter has cohered together from its diffuse
       float—and the soil is on the surface, and water runs,
       and vegetation sprouts,
For you only, and not for him and her?

7

A man's Body at auction;
I help the auctioneer—the sloven does not half know
       his business.

Gentlemen, look on this wonder!
Whatever the bids of the bidders, they cannot be high enough
       for it;
For it the globe lay preparing quintillions of years, without one
       animal or plant;
For it the revolving cycles truly and steadily roll'd.

In this head the all-baffling brain;
In it and below it, the makings of heroes.

Examine these limbs, red, black, or white—they are so cunning
       in tendon and nerve;
They shall be stript, that you may see them.

Exquisite senses, life-lit eyes, pluck, volition,
Flakes of breast-muscle, pliant back-bone and neck, flesh not
       flabby, good-sized arms and legs,
And wonders within there yet.

Within there runs blood,
The some old blood!
The some red-running blood!

There swells and jets a heart—there all passions, desires,
  reachings, aspirations;
Do you think they are not there because they are not express'd
  in parlors and lecture-rooms?

This is not only one man—this is the father of those who shall
  be fathers in their turns;
In him the start of populous states and rich republics;
Of him countless immortal lives, with countless embodiments
  and enjoyments.

How do you know who shall come from the offspring of his
  offspring through the centuries?
Who might you find you have come from yourself, if you
  could trace back through the centuries?

8

A woman's Body at auction!
She too is not only herself—she is the teeming mother
  of mothers;
She is the bearer of them that shall grow and be mates
  to the mothers.

Have you ever loved the Body of a woman?
Have you ever loved the Body of a man?
Your father—where is your father?
Your mother—is she living? have you been much with her?
  and has she been much with you?
—Do you not see that these are exactly the same to all, in all
  nations and times, all over the earth?

If any thing is sacred, the human body is sacred,
And the glory and sweet of a man, is the token of
       manhood untainted;
And in man or woman, a clean, strong, firm-fibred body, is
      beautiful as the most beautiful face.

Have you seen the foolthat corrupted his own live body?
For they do not conceal themselves, and cannot conceal
      themselves.

9

O my Body! I dare not desert the likes of you in other men
      and women, nor the likes of the parts of you;
I believe the likes of you are to stand or fall with the likes of
      the Soul, (and that they are the Soul;)
I believe the likes of you shall stand or fall with my poems—
      and that they are poems,
Man's, woman's, child's, youth's, wife's, husband's, mother's,
      father's, young man's, young woman's poems;
Head, neck, hair, ears, drop and tympan of the ears,
Eyes, eye-fringes, iris of the eye, eye-brows, and the waking or
      sleeping of the lids,
Mouth, tongue, lips, teeth, roof of the mouth, jaws, and the
      jaw-hinges,
Nose, nostrils of the nose, and the partition,
Cheeks, temples, forehead, chin, throat, back of the neck,
      neck-slue,
Strong shoulders, manly beard, scapula, hind-shoulders, and
      the ample side-round of the chest,
Upper-arm, arm-pit, elbow-socket, lower-arm, arm-sinews,
      arm-bones,
Wrist and wrist-joints, hand, palm, knuckles, thumb, fore-
      finger, finger-balls, finger-joints, finger nails,

Broad breast-front, curling hair of the breast, breast-bone,
      breast-side,
Ribs, belly, back-bone, joints of the back-bone,
Hips, hip-sockets, hip-strength, inward and outward round,
      man-balls, man-root,
Strong set of thighs, well carrying the trunk above,
Leg-fibres, knee, knee-pan, upper-leg, under leg,
Ankles, instep, foot-ball, toes, toe-joints, the heel;
All attitudes, all the shapeliness, all the belongings of my or
      your body, or of any one's body, male or female,
The lung-sponges, the stomach-sac, the bowels sweet
      and clean,
The brain in its folds inside the skull-frame,
Sympathies, heart-valves, palate-valves, sexuality, maternity,
Womanhood, and all that is a woman – and the man that
      comes from woman,
The womb, the teats, nipples, breast-milk, tears, laughter,
      weeping, love-looks, love-perturbations and risings,
The voice, articulation, language, whispering, shouting aloud,
Food, drink, pulse, digestion, sweat, sleep, walking, swimming,
Poise on the hips, leaping, reclining, embracing, arm-curving
      and tightening,
The continual changes of the flex of the mouth, and around
      the eyes,
The skin, the sun-burnt shade, freckles, hair,
The curious sympathy one feels, when feeling with the hand
      the naked meat of the body,
The circling rivers, the breath, and breathing it in and out,
The beauty of the waist, and thence of the hips, and thence
      downward toward the knees,
The thin red jellies within you, or within me – the bones, and
      the marrow in the bones,

The exquisite realization of health;
O I say, these are not the parts and poems of the Body only,
          but of the Soul,
O I say now these are the Soul!

In Paths Untrodden

First published in 1860

IN PATHS UNTRODDEN,
In the growth by margins of pond-waters,
Escaped from the life that exhibits itself,
From all the standards hitherto publish'd – from the pleasures,
          profits, eruditions, conformities,
Which too long I was offering to feed my soul;
Clear to me, now, standards not yet publish'd – clear to me that
          my Soul,
That the Soul of the man I speak for, feeds, rejoices most
          in comrades;
Here, by myself, away from the clank of the world,
Tallying and talk'd to here by tongues aromatic,
No longer abash'd – for in this secluded spot I can respond as I
          would not dare elsewhere,
Strong upon me the life that does not exhibit itself, yet
          contains all the rest,
Resolv'd to sing no songs to-day but those of manly
          attachment,
Projecting them along that substantial life,
Bequeathing, hence, types of athletic love,

Afternoon, this delicious Ninth-month, in my forty-first year,
I proceed, for all who are or have been young men,
To tell the secret of my nights and days,
To celebrate the need of comrades.

RECORDERS AGES HENCE

First published in 1860

RECORDERS AGES HENCE!
Come, I will take you down underneath this impassive
        exterior—I will tell you what to say of me;
Publish my name and hang up my picture as that of the
        tenderest lover,
The friend, the lover's portrait, of whom his friend, his lover,
        was fondest,
Who was not proud of his songs, but of the measureless ocean
        of love within him—and freely pour'd it forth,
Who often walk'd lonesome walks, thinking of his dear friends,
        his lovers,
Who pensive, away from one he lov'd, often lay sleepless and
        dissatisfied at night,
Who knew too well the sick, sick dread lest the one he lov'd
        might secretly be indifferent to him,
Whose happiest days were far away, through fields, in woods,
        on hills, he and another, wandering hand in hand, they
        twain, apart from other men,
Who oft as he saunter'd the streets, curv'd with his arm the
        shoulder of his friend—while the arm of his friend
        rested upon him also.

Salut au Monde!

First published in 1856

1

O TAKE MY hand, Walt Whitman!
Such gliding wonders! such sights and sounds!
Such join'd unended links, each hook'd to the next!
Each answering all – each sharing the earth with all.

What widens within you, Walt Whitman?
What waves and soils exuding?
What climes? what persons and lands are here?
Who are the infants? some playing, some slumbering?
Who are the girls? who are the married women?
Who are the groups of old men going slowly with their arms
        about each other's necks?
What rivers are these? what forests and fruits are these?
What are the mountains call'd that rise so high in the mists?
What myriads of dwellings are they, fill'd with dwellers?

2

Within me latitude widens, longitude lengthens;
Asia, Africa, Europe, are to the east – America is provided for in
        the west;
Banding the bulge of the earth winds the hot equator,
Curiously north and south turn the axis-ends;
Within me is the longest day – the sun wheels in slanting
        rings – it does not set for months;
Stretch'd in due time within me the midnight sun just rises
        above the horizon, and sinks again;

Within me zones, seas, cataracts, plants, volcanoes, groups,
Malaysia, Polynesia, and the great West Indian islands.

3

What do you hear, Walt Whitman?

I hear the workman singing, and the farmer's wife singing;
I hear in the distance the sounds of children, and of animals
      early in the day;
I hear quick rifle-cracks from the riflemen of East Tennessee
      and Kentucky, hunting on hills;
I hear emulous shouts of Australians, pursuing the wild horse;
I hear the Spanish dance, with castanets, in the chestnut
      shade, to the rebeck and guitar;
I hear continual echoes from the Thames;
I hear fierce French liberty songs;
I hear of the Italian boat-sculler the musical recitative
      of old poems;
I hear the Virginia plantation-chorus of negroes, of a harvest
      night, in the glare of pine-knots;
I hear the strong baritone of the long-shore-men of
      Mannahatta;
I hear the stevedores unlading the cargoes, and singing;
I hear the screams of the water-fowl of solitary north-
      west lakes;
I hear the rustling pattering of locusts, as they strike the grain
      and grass with the showers of their terrible clouds;
I hear the Coptic refrain, toward sundown, pensively falling on
      the breast of the black venerable vast mother, the Nile;
I hear the bugles of raft-tenders on the streams of Kanada;

I hear the chirp of the Mexican muleteer, and the bells
      of the mule;
I hear the Arab muezzin, calling from the top of the mosque;
I hear the Christian priests at the altars of their churches—I
      hear the responsive bass and soprano;
I hear the wail of utter despair of the white-hair'd Irish
      grandparents, when they learn the death of
      their grandson;
I hear the cry of the Cossack, and the sailor's voice, putting to
      sea at Okotsk;
I hear the wheeze of the slave-coffle, as the slaves march on—
      as the husky gangs pass on by twos and threes, fasten'd
      together with wrist-chains and ankle-chains;
I hear the entreaties of women tied up for punishment—I hear
      the sibilant whisk of throngs through the air;
I hear the Hebrew reading his records and psalms;
I hear the rhythmic myths of the Greeks, and the strong
      legends of the Romans;
I hear the tale of the divine life and bloody death of the
      beautiful God—the Christ;
I hear the Hindoo teaching his favorite pupil the loves, wars,
      adages, transmitted safely to this day, from poets who
      wrote three thousand years ago.

4

What do you see, Walt Whitman?
Who are they you salute, and that one after another salute
      you?

I see a great round wonder rolling through the air;
I see diminute farms, hamlets, ruins, grave-yards, jails,
      factories, palaces, hovels, huts of barbarians, tents of
      nomads, upon the surface;

I see the shaded part on one side, where the sleepers are
       sleeping—and the sun-lit part of the other side,
I see the curious silent change of the light and shade,
I see distant lands, as real and near to the inhabitants of them,
       as my land is to me.

I see plenteous waters;
I see mountain peaks—I see the sierras of Andes and
       Alleghanies, where they range;
I see plainly the Himalayas, Chian Shahs, Altays, Ghauts;
I see the giant pinnacles of Elbruz, Kazbek, Bazardjusi,
I see the Rocky Mountains, and the Peak of Winds;
I see the Styrian Alps, and the Karnac Alps;
I see the Pyrenees, Balks, Carpathians—and to the north the
       Dofrafields, and off at sea Mount Hecla;
I see Vesuvius and Etna—I see the Anahuacs;
I see the Mountains of the Moon, and the Snow Mountains,
       and the Red Mountains of Madagascar;
I see the Vermont hills, and the long string of Cordilleras;
I see the vast deserts of Western America;
I see the Lybian, Arabian, and Asiatic deserts;
I see huge dreadful Arctic and Antarctic icebergs;
I see the superior oceans and the inferior ones—the Atlantic
       and Pacific, the sea of Mexico, the Brazilian sea, and
       the sea of Peru,
The Japan waters, those of Hindostan, the China Sea, and the
       Gulf of Guinea,
The spread of the Baltic, Caspian, Bothnia, the British shores,
       and the Bay of Biscay,
The clear-sunn'd Mediterranean, and from one to another
       of its islands,

The inland fresh-tasted seas of North America,
The White Sea, and the sea around Greenland.

I behold the mariners of the world;
Some are in storms—some in the night, with the watch on the
       look-out;
Some drifting helplessly—some with contagious diseases.

I behold the sail and steamships of the world, some in clusters
       in port, some on their voyages;
Some double the Cape of Storms—some Cape Verde,—others
       Cape Guardafui, Bon, or Bajadore;
Others Dondra Head—others pass the Straits of Sunda—others
       Cape Lopatka—others Behring's Straits;
Others Cape Horn—others sail the Gulf of Mexico, or along
       Cuba or Hayti—others Hudson's Bay or Baffin's Bay;
Others pass the Straits of Dover—others enter the Wash—
       others the Firth of Solway—others round Cape Clear—
       others the Land's End;
Others traverse the Zuyder Zee, or the Scheld;
Others add to the exits and entrances at Sandy Hook;
Others to the comers and goers at Gibraltar, or the
       Dardanelles;
Others sternly push their way through the northern
       winter-packs;
Others descend or ascend the Obi or the Lena;
Others the Niger or the Congo—others the Indus, the
       Burampooter and Cambodia;
Others wait at the wharves of Manhattan, steam'd up, ready
       to start;
Wait, swift and swarthy, in the ports of Australia;

Wait at Liverpool, Glasgow, Dublin, Marseilles, Lisbon, Naples,
        Hamburg, Bremen, Bordeaux, the Hague, Copenhagen;
Wait at Valparaiso, Rio Janeiro, Panama;
Wait at their moorings at Boston, Philadelphia, Baltimore,
        Charleston, New Orleans, Galveston, San Francisco.

5

I see the tracks of the rail-roads of the earth;
I see them welding State to State, city to city, through
        North America;
I see them in Great Britain, I see them in Europe;
I see them in Asia and in Africa.

I see the electric telegraphs of the earth;
I see the filaments of the news of the wars, deaths, losses,
        gains, passions, of my race.

I see the long river-stripes of the earth;
I see where the Mississippi flows—I see where the
        Columbia flows;
I see the Great River and the Falls of Niagara;
I see the Amazon and the Paraguay;
I see the four great rivers of China, the Amour, the Yellow
        River, the Yiang-tse, and the Pearl;
I see where the Seine flows, and where the Danube, the Loire,
        the Rhone, and the Guadalquiver flow;
I see the windings of the Volga, the Dnieper, the Oder;
I see the Tuscan going down the Arno, and the Venetian
        along the Po;
I see the Greek seaman sailing out of Egina bay.

6

I see the site of the old empire of Assyria, and that of Persia,
      and that of India;
I see the falling of the Ganges over the high rim of Saukara.

I see the place of the idea of the Deity incarnated by avatars in
      human forms;
I see the spots of the successions of priests on the earth —
      oracles, sacrificers, brahmins, sabians, lamas, monks,
      muftis, exhorters;
I see where druids walked the groves of Mona — I see the
      mistle-toe and vervain;
I see the temples of the deaths of the bodies of Gods — I see the
      old signifiers.

I see Christ once more eating the bread of his last supper, in
      the midst of youths and old persons;
I see where the strong divine young man, the Hercules, toil'd
      faithfully and long, and then died;
I see the place of the innocent rich life and hapless fate of the
      beautiful nocturnal son, the full-limb'd Bacchus;
I see Kneph, blooming, drest in blue, with the crown of
      feathers on his head;
I see Hermes, unsuspected, dying, well-beloved, saying to the
      people, *Do not weep for me,*
This is not my true country, I have lived banish'd from my true
      country — I now go back there,
I return to the celestial sphere, where every one goes in his turn.

7

I see the battle-fields of the earth – grass grows upon them, and
     blossoms and corn;
I see the tracks of ancient and modern expeditions.

I see the nameless masonries, venerable messages of the
     unknown events, heroes, records of the earth.

I see the places of the sagas;
I see pine-trees and fir-trees torn by northern blasts;
I see granite boulders and cliffs – I see green meadows
     and lakes;
I see the burial-cairns of Scandinavian warriors;
I see them raised high with stones, by the marge of restless
     oceans, that the dead men's spirits, when they wearied
     of their quiet graves, might rise up through the
     mounds, and gaze on the tossing billows, and be
     refresh'd by storms, immensity, liberty, action.

I see the steppes of Asia;
I see the tumuli of Mongolia – I see the tents of Kalmucks
     and Baskirs;
I see the nomadic tribes, with herds of oxen and cows;
I see the table-lands notch'd with ravines – I see the jungles and
     deserts;
I see the camel, the wild steed, the bustard, the fat-tail'd sheep,
     the antelope, and the burrowing wolf.

I see the high-lands of Abyssinia;
I see flocks of goats feeding, and see the fig-tree,
     tamarind, date,

And see fields of teff-wheat, and see the places of verdure
          and gold.

I see the Brazilian vaquero;
I see the Bolivian ascending Mount Sorata;
I see the Wacho crossing the plains—I see the incomparable
          rider of horses with his lasso on his arm;
I see over the pampas the pursuit of wild cattle for their hides.

8

I see little and large sea-dots, some inhabited, some
          uninhabited;
I see two boats with nets, lying off the shore of Paumanok,
          quite still;
I see ten fishermen waiting—they discover now a thick school
          of mossbonkers—they drop the join'd seine-ends
          in the water,
The boats separate—they diverge and row off, each on its
          rounding course to the beach, enclosing the
          mossbonkers;
The net is drawn in by a windlass by those who stop ashore,
Some of the fishermen lounge in their boats—others stand
          negligently ankle-deep in the water, pois'd on
          strong legs;
The boats are partly drawn up—the water slaps against them;
On the sand, in heaps and winrows, well out from the water,
          lie the green-back'd spotted mossbonkers.

9

I see the despondent red man in the west, lingering about the
          banks of Moingo, and about Lake Pepin;
He has heard the quail and beheld the honey-bee, and sadly
          prepared to depart.

I see the regions of snow and ice;
I see the sharp-eyed Samoiede and the Finn;
I see the seal-seeker in his boat, poising his lance;
I see the Siberian on his slight-built sledge, drawn by dogs;
I see the porpoise-hunters—I see the whale-crews of the South
      Pacific and the North Atlantic;
I see the cliffs, glaciers, torrents, valleys, of Switzerland—I mark
      the long winters, and the isolation.

I see the cities of the earth, and make myself at random a
      part of them;
I am a real Parisian;
I am a habitan of Vienna, St. Petersburg, Berlin, Constantinople;
I am of Adelaide, Sidney, Melbourne;
I am of London, Manchester, Bristol, Edinburgh, Limerick;
I am of Madrid, Cadiz, Barcelona, Oporto, Lyons, Brussels,
      Berne, Frankfort, Stuttgart, Turin, Florence;
I belong in Moscow, Cracow, Warsaw—or northward in
      Christiania or Stockholm—or in Siberian Irkutsk—or in
      some street in Iceland;
I descend upon all those cities, and rise from them again.

10

I see vapors exhaling from unexplored countries;
I see the savage types, the bow and arrow, the poison'd splint,
      the fetish, and the obi.

I see African and Asiatic towns;
I see Algiers, Tripoli, Derne, Mogadore, Timbuctoo, Monrovia;
I see the swarms of Pekin, Canton, Benares, Delhi, Calcutta, Yedo;

I see the Kruman in his hut, and the Dahoman and
        Ashanteeman in their huts;
I see the Turk smoking opium in Aleppo;
I see the picturesque crowds at the fairs of Khiva, and
        those of Herat;
I see Teheran—I see Muscat and Medina, and the intervening
        sands—I see the caravans toiling onward;
I see Egypt and the Egyptians—I see the pyramids
        and obelisks;
I look on chisel'd histories, songs, philosophies, cut in slabs of
        sand-stone, or on granite-blocks;
I see at Memphis mummy-pits, containing mummies,
        embalm'd, swathed in linen cloth, lying there
        many centuries;
I look on the fall'n Theban, the large-ball'd eyes, the side-
        drooping neck, the hands folded across the breast.

I see the menials of the earth, laboring;
I see the prisoners in the prisons;
I see the defective human bodies of the earth;
I see the blind, the deaf and dumb, idiots, hunchbacks,
        lunatics;
I see the pirates, thieves, betrayers, murderers, slave-makers
        of the earth;
I see the helpless infants, and the helpless old men
        and women.

I see male and female everywhere;
I see the serene brotherhood of philosophs;
I see the constructiveness of my race;
I see the results of the perseverance and industry of my race;

I see ranks, colors, barbarisms, civilizations—I go among
     them—I mix indiscriminately,
And I salute all the inhabitants of the earth.

11

You, whoever you are!
You daughter or son of England!
You of the mighty Slavic tribes and empires! you Russ
     in Russia!
You dim-descended, black, divine soul'd African, large, fine-
     headed, nobly-form'd, superbly destin'd, on equal terms
     with me!
You Norwegian! Swede! Dane! Icelander! you Prussian!
You Spaniard of Spain! you Portuguese!
You Frenchwoman and Frenchman of France!
You Belge! you liberty-lover of the Netherlands!
You sturdy Austrian! you Lombard! Hun! Bohemian! farmer
     of Styria!
You neighbor of the Danube!
You working-man of the Rhine, the Elbe, or the Weser! you
     working-woman too!
You Sardinian! you Bavarian! Swabian! Saxon! Wallachian!
     Bulgarian!
You citizen of Prague! Roman! Neapolitan! Greek!
You lithe matador in the arena at Seville!
You mountaineer living lawlessly on the Taurus or Caucasus!
You Bokh horse-herd, watching your mares and stallions
     feeding!
You beautiful-bodied Persian, at full speed in the saddle,
     shooting arrows to the mark!

You Chinaman and Chinawoman of China! you Tartar
      of Tartary!
You women of the earth subordinated at your tasks!
You Jew journeying in your old age through every risk, to stand
      once on Syrian ground!
You other Jews waiting in all lands for your Messiah!
You thoughtful Armenian, pondering by some stream of the
      Euphrates! you peering amid the ruins of Nineveh! you
      ascending Mount Ararat!
You foot-worn pilgrim welcoming the far-away sparkle of the
      minarets of Mecca!
You sheiks along the stretch from Suez to Bab-el-mandeb,
      ruling your families and tribes!
You olive-grower tending your fruit on fields of Nazareth,
      Damascus, or Lake Tiberias!
You Thibet trader on the wide inland, or bargaining in the
      shops of Lassa!
You Japanese man or woman! you liver in Madagascar, Ceylon,
      Sumatra, Borneo!
All you on the numberless islands of the archipelagoes
      of the sea!
And you of centuries hence, when you listen to me!
And you, each and everywhere, whom I specify not, but
      include just the same!
Health to you! Good will to you all – from me and America sent.

Each of us inevitable;
Each of us limitless – each of us with his or her right
      upon the earth;
Each of us allow'd the eternal purports of the earth;
Each of us here as divinely as any is here.

12

You Hottentot with clicking palate! You woolly-hair'd hordes!
You own'd persons, dropping sweat-drops or blood-drops!
You human forms with the fathomless ever-impressive
      countenances of brutes!
I dare not refuse you — the scope of the world, and of time and
      space, are upon me.

You poor koboo whom the meanest of the rest look down
      upon, for all your glimmering language and
      spirituality!
You low expiring aborigines of the hills of Utah, Oregon,
      California!
You dwarf'd Kamtschatkan, Greenlander, Lapp!
You Austral negro, naked, red, sooty, with protrusive lip,
      grovelling, seeking your food!
You Caffre, Berber, Soudanese!
You haggard, uncouth, untutor'd, Bedowee!
You plague-swarms in Madras, Nankin, Kaubul, Cairo!
You bather bathing in the Ganges!
You benighted roamer of Amazonia! you Patagonian!
      you Fejee-man!
You peon of Mexico! you slave of Carolina, Texas, Tennessee!
I do not prefer others so very much before you either;
I do not say one word against you, away back there,
      where you stand;
(You will come forward in due time to my side.)

My spirit has pass'd in compassion and determination around
      the whole earth;

I have look'd for equals and lovers, and found them ready for
      me in all lands;
I think some divine rapport has equalized me with them.

13

O vapors! I think I have risen with you, and moved away to
      distant continents, and fallen down there, for reasons;
I think I have blown with you, O winds;
O waters, I have finger'd every shore with you.

I have run though what any river or strait of the globe has
      run through;
I have taken my stand on the bases of peninsulas, and on the
      high embedded rocks, to cry thence.

Salut au monde!
What cities the light or warmth penetrates, I penetrate those
      cities myself;
All islands to which birds wing their way, I wing my
      way myself.

Toward all,
I raise high the perpendicular hand – I make the signal,
To remain after me in sight forever,
For all the haunts and homes of men.

AMERICAN FEUILLAGE

First published in 1860

AMERICA ALWAYS!
Always our own feuillage!

Always Florida's green peninsula! Always the priceless delta
of Louisiana! Always the cotton-fields of Alabama
and Texas!

Always California's golden hills and hollows—and the silver
mountains of New Mexico! Always soft-breath'd Cuba!

Always the vast slope drain'd by the Southern Sea—inseparable
with the slopes drain'd by the Eastern and
Western Seas;

The area the eighty-third year of These States—the three and a
half millions of square miles;

The eighteen thousand miles of sea-coast and bay-coast on the
main—the thirty thousand miles of river navigation,

The seven millions of distinct families, and the same number
of dwellings—Always these, and more, branching forth
into numberless branches;

Always the free range and diversity! always the continent
of Democracy!

Always the prairies, pastures, forests, vast cities, travelers,
Kanada, the snows;

Always these compact lands—lands tied at the hips with the
belt stringing the huge oval lakes;

Always the West, with strong native persons—the increasing
density there—the habitans, friendly, threatening,
ironical, scorning invaders;

All sights, South, North, East—all deeds, promiscuously
done at all times,

All characters, movements, growths—a few noticed,
myriads unnoticed,

Through Mannahatta's streets I walking, these things gathering;

On interior rivers, by night, in the glare of pine knots,
steamboats wooding up;

Sunlight by day on the valley of the Susquehanna, and on the
       valleys of the Potomac and Rappahannock, and the
       valleys of the Roanoke and Delaware;
In their northerly wilds, beasts of prey haunting the
       Adirondacks, the hills–or lapping the Saginaw waters
       to drink;
In a lonesome inlet, a sheldrake, lost from the flock, sitting on
       the water, rocking silently;
In farmers' barns, oxen in the stable, their harvest labor done–
       they rest standing–they are too tired;
Afar on arctic ice, the she-walrus lying drowsily, while her
       cubs play around;
The hawk sailing where men have not yet sail'd–the farthest
       polar sea, ripply, crystalline, open, beyond the floes;
White drift spooning ahead, where the ship in the
       tempest dashes;
On solid land, what is done in cities, as the bells all strike
       midnight together;
In primitive woods, the sounds there also sounding–the howl
       of the wolf, the scream of the panther, and the hoarse
       bellow of the elk;
In winter beneath the hard blue ice of Moosehead Lake–in
       summer visible through the clear waters, the great
       trout swimming;
In lower latitudes, in warmer air, in the Carolinas, the large
       black buzzard floating slowly, high beyond the
       tree tops,
Below, the red cedar, festoon'd with tylandria–the pines and
       cypresses, growing out of the white sand that spreads
       far and flat;

Rude boats descending the big Pedee – climbing plants,
       parasites, with color'd flowers and berries, enveloping
       huge trees,
The waving drapery on the live oak, trailing long and low,
       noiselessly waved by the wind;
The camp of Georgia wagoners, just after dark – the
       supper-fires, and the cooking and eating by whites
       and negroes,
Thirty or forty great wagons – the mules, cattle, horses, feeding
       from troughs,
The shadows, gleams, up under the leaves of the old sycamore-
       trees – the flames – with the black smoke from the
       pitch-pine, curling and rising;
Southern fishermen fishing – the sounds and inlets of North
       Carolina's coast – the shad-fishery and the herring-
       fishery – the large sweep-seines – the windlasses on
       shore work'd by horses – the clearing, curing, and
       packing-houses;
Deep in the forest, in piney woods, turpentine dropping from
       the incisions in the trees – There are the turpentine works,
There are the negroes at work, in good health – the ground in
       all directions is cover'd with pine straw:
– In Tennessee and Kentucky, slaves busy in the coalings,
       at the forge, by the furnace-blaze, or at the
       corn-shucking;
In Virginia, the planter's son returning after a long absence,
       joyfully welcom'd and kiss'd by the aged mulatto nurse;
On rivers, boatmen safely moor'd at night-fall, in their boats,
       under shelter of high banks,

Some of the younger men dance to the sound of the banjo
        or fiddle – others sit on the gunwale, smoking
        and talking;
Late in the afternoon, the mocking-bird, the American mimic,
        singing in the Great Dismal Swamp – there are the
        greenish waters, the resinous odor, the plenteous moss,
        the cypress tree, and the juniper tree;
– Northward, young men of Mannahatta – the target company
        from an excursion returning home at evening – the
        musket-muzzles all bear bunches of flowers presented
        by women;
Children at play – or on his father's lap a young boy fallen
        asleep, (how his lips move! how he smiles in
        his sleep!)
The scout riding on horse back over the plains west of the
        Mississippi – he ascends a knoll and sweeps his
        eye around;
California life – the miner, bearded, dress'd in his rude
        costume – the stanch California friendship – the sweet
        air – the graves one, in passing, meets, solitary, just
        aside the horsepath;
Down in Texas, the cotton-field, the negro-cabins – drivers
        driving mules or oxen before rude carts – cotton bales
        piled on banks and wharves;
Encircling all, vast-darting, up and wide, the American Soul,
        with equal hemispheres – one Love, one Dilation
        or Pride;
– In arriere, the peace-talk with the Iroquois, the aborigines –
        the calumet, the pipe of good-will, arbitration,
        and indorsement,

The sachem blowing the smoke first toward the sun and then
            toward the earth,
The drama of the scalp-dance enacted with painted faces and
            guttural exclamations,
The setting out of the war-party–the long and stealthy march,
The single-file–the swinging hatchets–the surprise and
            slaughter of enemies;
–All the acts, scenes, ways, persons, attitudes of These States
            –reminiscences, all institutions,
All These States, compact–Every square mile of These States,
            without excepting a particle–you also–me also,
Me pleas'd, rambling in lanes and country fields,
            Paumanok's fields,
Me, observing the spiral flight of two little yellow butterflies,
            shuffling between each other, ascending high
            in the air;
The darting swallow, the destroyer of insects–the fall traveler
            southward, but returning northward early
            in the spring;
The country boy at the close of the day, driving the herd of
            cows, and shouting to them as they loiter to browse by
            the road-side;
The city wharf–Boston, Philadelphia, Baltimore, Charleston,
            New Orleans, San Francisco,
The departing ships, when the sailors heave at the capstan;
–Evening–me in my room–the setting sun,
The setting summer sun shining in my open window, showing
            the swarm of flies, suspended, balancing in the air in
            the centre of the room, darting athwart, up and down,
            casting swift shadows in specks on the opposite wall,
            where the shine is;

The athletic American matron speaking in public to crowds
of listeners;
Males, females, immigrants, combinations – the copiousness –
the individuality of The States, each for itself – the
money-makers;
Factories, machinery, the mechanical forces – the windlass,
lever, pulley – All certainties,
The certainty of space, increase, freedom, futurity,
In space, the sporades, the scatter'd islands, the stars – on the
firm earth, the lands, my lands;
O lands! all so dear to me – what you are, (whatever it is,) I
become a part of that, whatever it is;
Southward there, I screaming, with wings slowly flapping, with
the myriads of gulls wintering along the coasts of
Florida – or in Louisiana, with pelicans breeding;
Otherways, there, atwixt the banks of the Arkansaw, the Rio
Grande, the Nueces, the Brazos, the Tombigbee, the
Red River, the Saskatchawan, or the Osage, I with the
spring waters laughing and skipping and running;
Northward, on the sands, on some shallow bay of Paumanok, I,
with parties of snowy herons wading in the wet to seek
worms and aquatic plants;
Retreating, triumphantly twittering, the king-bird, from
piercing the crow with its bill, for amusement – And I
triumphantly twittering;
The migrating flock of wild geese alighting in autumn to
refresh themselves – the body of the flock feed – the
sentinels outside move around with erect heads
watching, and are from time to time reliev'd by other
sentinels – And I feeding and taking turns with the rest;

In Kanadian forests, the moose, large as an ox, corner'd by
hunters, rising desperately on his hind-feet, and
plunging with his fore-feet, the hoofs as sharp as
knives—And I, plunging at the hunters, corner'd
and desperate;
In the Mannahatta, streets, piers, shipping, store-houses, and
the countless workmen working in the shops,
And I too of the Mannahatta, singing thereof—and no less in
myself than the whole of the Mannahatta in itself,
Singing the song of These, my ever-united lands—my body no
more inevitably united, part to part, and made one
identity, any more than my lands are inevitably united,
and made ONE IDENTITY;
Nativities, climates, the grass of the great Pastoral Plains;
Cities, labors, death, animals, products, war, good and evil—
these me,
These affording, in all their particulars, endless feuillage to me
and to America, how can I do less than pass the clew
of the union of them, to afford the like to you?
Whoever you are! how can I but offer you divine leaves, that
you also be eligible as I am?
How can I but, as here, chanting, invite you for yourself to
collect bouquets of the incomparable feuillage of
These States?

Song of the Broad-Axe

First published in 1856

1

Weapon, shapely, naked, wan!
Head from the mother's bowels drawn!
Wooded flesh and metal bone! limb only one, and lip
        only one!
Gray-blue leaf by red-heat grown! helve produced from a little
        seed sown!
Resting the grass amid and upon,
To be lean'd, and to lean on.

Strong shapes, and attributes of strong shapes—masculine
        trades, sights and sounds;
Long varied train of an emblem, dabs of music;
Fingers of the organist skipping staccato over the keys of the
        great organ.

2

Welcome are all earth's lands, each for its kind;
Welcome are lands of pine and oak;
Welcome are lands of the lemon and fig;
Welcome are lands of gold;
Welcome are lands of wheat and maize—welcome those
        of the grape;
Welcome are lands of sugar and rice;
Welcome the cotton-lands—welcome those of the white potato
        and sweet potato;
Welcome are mountains, flats, sands, forests, prairies;
Welcome the rich borders of rivers, table-lands, openings;

Welcome the measureless grazing-lands – welcome the teeming
          soil of orchards, flax, honey, hemp;
Welcome just as much the other more hard-faced lands;
Lands rich as lands of gold, or, wheat and fruit lands;
Lands of mines, lands of the manly and rugged ores;
Lands of coal, copper, lead, tin, zinc;
LANDS OF IRON! lands of the make of the axe!

3

The log at the wood-pile, the axe supported by it;
The sylvan hut, the vine over the doorway, the space clear'd for
          a garden,
The irregular tapping of rain down on the leaves, after the
          storm is lull'd,
The wailing and moaning at intervals, the thought of the sea,
The thought of ships struck in the storm, and put on their
          beam ends, and the cutting away of masts;
The sentiment of the huge timbers of old-fashion'd houses
          and barns;
The remember'd print or narrative, the voyage at a venture of
          men, families, goods,
The disembarkation, the founding of a new city,
The voyage of those who sought a New England and found
          it – the outset anywhere,
The settlements of the Arkansas, Colorado, Ottawa,
          Willamette,
The slow progress, the scant fare, the axe, rifle, saddle-bags;
The beauty of all adventurous and daring persons,
The beauty of wood-boys and wood-men, with their clear
          untrimm'd faces,

The beauty of independence, departure, actions that rely
      on themselves,
The American contempt for statutes and ceremonies, the
      boundless impatience of restraint,
The loose drift of character, the inkling through random types,
      the solidification;
The butcher in the slaughter-house, the hands aboard
      schooners and sloops, the raftsman, the pioneer,
Lumbermen in their winter camp, day-break in the woods,
      stripes of snow on the limbs of trees, the occasional
      snapping,
The glad clear sound of one's own voice, the merry song, the
      natural life of the woods, the strong day's work,
The blazing fire at night, the sweet taste of supper, the talk, the
      bed of hemlock boughs, and the bear-skin;
—The house-builder at work in cities or anywhere,
The preparatory jointing, squaring, sawing, mortising,
The hoist-up of beams, the push of them in their places, laying
      them regular,
Setting the studs by their tenons in the mortises, according as
      they were prepared,
The blows of mallets and hammers, the attitudes of the men,
      their curv'd limbs,
Bending, standing, astride the beams, driving in pins, holding
      on by posts and braces,
The hook'd arm over the plate, the other arm wielding the axe,
The floor-men forcing the planks close, to be nail'd,
Their postures bringing their weapons downward on
      the bearers,
The echoes resounding through the vacant building;
The huge store-house carried up in the city, well under way,

The six framing-men, two in the middle, and two at each end,
  carefully bearing on their shoulders a heavy stick for
  a cross-beam,
The crowded line of masons with trowels in their right hands,
  rapidly laying the long side-wall, two hundred feet
  from front to rear,
The flexible rise and fall of backs, the continual click of the
  trowels striking the bricks,
The bricks, one after another, each laid so workmanlike in its
  place, and set with a knock of the trowel-handle,
The piles of materials, the mortar on the mortar-boards, and
  the steady replenishing by the hod-men;
—Spar-makers in the spar-yard, the swarming row of well-
  grown apprentices,
The swing of their axes in the square-hew'd log, shaping it
  toward the shape of a mast,
The brisk short crackle of the steel driven slantingly into
  the pine,
The butter-color'd chips flying off in great flakes and slivers,
The limber motion of brawny young arms and hips in
  easy costumes;
The constructor of wharves, bridges, piers, bulk-heads, floats,
  stays against the sea;
—The city fireman—the fire that suddenly bursts forth in the
  close-pack'd square,
The arriving engines, the hoarse shouts, the nimble stepping
  and daring,
The strong command through the fire-trumpets, the falling in
  line, the rise and fall of the arms forcing the water,
The slender, spasmic, blue-white jets—the bringing to bear of
  the hooks and ladders, and their execution,

The crash and cut away of connecting wood-work, or through
        floors, if the fire smoulders under them,
The crowd with their lit faces, watching – the glare and
        dense shadows;
–The forger at his forge-furnace, and the user of iron
        after him,
The maker of the axe large and small, and the welder
        and temperer,
The chooser breathing his breath on the cold steel, and trying
        the edge with his thumb,
The one who clean-shapes the handle, and sets it firmly
        in the socket;
The shadowy processions of the portraits of the past
        users also,
The primal patient mechanics, the architects and engineers,
The far-off Assyrian edifice and Mizra edifice,
The Roman lictors preceding the consuls,
The antique European warrior with his axe in combat,
The uplifted arm, the clatter of blows on the helmeted head,
The death-howl, the limpsey tumbling body, the rush of friend
        and foe thither,
The siege of revolted lieges determin'd for liberty,
The summons to surrender, the battering at castle gates, the
        truce and parley;
The sack of an old city in its time,
The bursting in of mercenaries and bigots tumultuously
        and disorderly,
Roar, flames, blood, drunkenness, madness,
Goods freely rifled from houses and temples, screams of
        women in the gripe of brigands,

Craft and thievery of camp-followers, men running, old
      persons despairing,
The hell of war, the cruelties of creeds,
The list of all executive deeds and words, just or unjust,
The power of personality, just or unjust.

4

Muscle and pluck forever!
What invigorates life, invigorates death,
And the dead advance as much as the living advance,
And the future is no more uncertain than the present,
And the roughness of the earth and of man encloses as much
      as the delicatesse of the earth and of man,
And nothing endures but personal qualities.

What do you think endures?
Do you think the great city endures?
Or a teeming manufacturing state? or a prepared constitution?
      or the best-built steamships?
Or hotels of granite and iron? or any chef-d'œuvres of
      engineering, forts, armaments?

Away! These are not to be cherish'd for themselves;
They fill their hour, the dancers dance, the musicians
      play for them;
The show passes, all does well enough of course,
All does very well till one flash of defiance.

The great city is that which has the greatest man or woman;
If it be a few ragged huts, it is still the greatest city in the
      whole world.

5

The place where the great city stands is not the place of
stretch'd wharves, docks, manufactures, deposits
of produce,
Nor the place of ceaseless salutes of new comers, or the
anchor-lifters of the departing,
Nor the place of the tallest and costliest buildings, or shops
selling goods from the rest of the earth,
Nor the place of the best libraries and schools—nor the place
where money is plentiest,
Nor the place of the most numerous population.

Where the city stands with the brawniest breed of orators
and bards;
Where the city stands that is beloved by these, and loves them
in return, and understands them;
Where no monuments exist to heroes, but in the common
words and deeds;
Where thrift is in its place, and prudence is in its place;
Where the men and women think lightly of the laws;
Where the slave ceases, and the master of slaves ceases;
Where the populace rise at once against the never-ending
audacity of elected persons;
Where fierce men and women pour forth, as the sea to the
whistle of death pours its sweeping and unript waves;
Where outside authority enters always after the precedence of
inside authority;
Where the citizen is always the head and ideal—and President,
Mayor, Governor, and what not, are agents for pay;
Where children are taught to be laws to themselves, and to
depend on themselves;

Where equanimity is illustrated in affairs;
Where speculations on the Soul are encouraged;
Where women walk in public processions in the streets, the
      same as the men,
Where they enter the public assembly and take places the
      same as the men;
Where the city of the faithfulest friends stands;
Where the city of the cleanliness of the sexes stands;
Where the city of the healthiest fathers stands;
Where the city of the best-bodied mothers stands,
There the great city stands.

6

How beggarly appear arguments before a defiant deed!
How the floridness of the materials of cities shrivels before a
      man's or woman's look!

All waits, or goes by default, till a strong being appears;
A strong being is the proof of the race, and of the ability
      of the universe;
When he or she appears, materials are overaw'd,
The dispute on the Soul stops,
The old customs and phrases are confronted, turn'd back,
      or laid away.

What is your money-making now? what can it do now?
What is your respectability now?
What are your theology, tuition, society, traditions, statute-
      books, now?
Where are your jibes of being now?
Where are your cavils about the Soul now?

7

A sterile landscape covers the ore – there is as good as the best,
  for all the forbidding appearance;
There is the mine, there are the miners;
The forge-furnace is there, the melt is accomplish'd; the
   hammers-men are at hand with their tongs
   and hammers;
What always served, and always serves, is at hand.

Than this, nothing has better served – it has served all:
Served the fluent-tongued and subtle-sensed Greek, and long
  ere the Greek:
Served in building the buildings that last longer than any;
Served the Hebrew, the Persian, the most ancient Hindostanee;
Served the mound-raiser on the Mississippi – served those
  whose relics remain in Central America;
Served Albic temples in woods or on plains, with unhewn
  pillars, and the druids;
Served the artificial clefts, vast, high, silent, on the snow-
  cover'd hills of Scandinavia;
Served those who, time out mind, made on the granite walls
  rough sketches of the sun, moon, stars, ships,
  ocean-waves;
Served the paths of the irruptions of the Goths – served the
  pastoral tribes and nomads;
Served the long, long distant Kelt – served the hardy pirates of
  the Baltic;
Served before any of those, the venerable and harmless men
  of Ethiopia;
Served the making of helms for the galleys of pleasure, and the
  making of those for war;

Served all great works on land, and all great works on the sea;
For the mediæval ages; and before the medival ages;
Served not the living only, then as now, but served the dead.

8

I see the European headsman;
He stands mask'd, clothed in red, with huge legs, and strong
          naked arms,
And leans on a ponderous axe.

(Whom have you slaughter'd lately, European headsman?
Whose is that blood upon you, so wet and sticky?)

I see the clear sunsets of the martyrs;
I see from the scaffolds the descending ghosts,
Ghosts of dead lords, uncrown'd ladies, impeach'd ministers,
          rejected kings,
Rivals, traitors, poisoners, disgraced chieftains, and the rest.

I see those who in any land have died for the good cause;
The seed is spare, nevertheless the crop shall never
          run out;
(Mind you, O foreign kings, O priests, the crop shall never
          run out.)

I see the blood wash'd entirely away from the axe;
Both blade and helve are clean;
They spirt no more the blood of European nobles—they clasp
          no more the necks of queens.

I see the headsman withdraw and become useless;
I see the scaffold untrodden and mouldy–I wee no longer any
          axe upon it;
I see the mighty and friendly emblem of the power of my own
          race–the newest, largest race.

9

(America! I do not vaunt my love for you;
I have what I have.)
The axe leaps!
The solid forest gives fluid utterances;
They tumble forth, they rise and form,
Hut, tent, landing, survey,
Flail, plough, pick, crowbar, spade,
Shingle, rail, prop, wainscot, jamb, lath, panel, gable,
Citadel, ceiling, saloon, academy, organ, exhibition-house,
          library,
Cornice, trellis, pilaster, balcony, window, shutter, turret, porch,
Hoe, rake, pitch-fork, pencil, wagon, staff, saw, jack-plane,
          mallet, wedge, rounce,
Chair, tub, hoop, table, wicket, vane, sash, floor,
Work-box, chest, string'd instrument, boat, frame, and
          what not,
Capitols of States, and capitol of the nation of States,
Long stately rows in avenues, hospitals for orphans, or for the
          poor or sick,
Manhattan steamboats and clippers, taking the measure of
          all seas.

The shapes arise!
Shapes of the using of axes anyhow, and the users, and all that
          neighbors them,

Cutters down of wood, and haulers of it to the Penobscot
    or Kennebec,
Dwellers in cabins among the California mountains, or by the
    little lakes, or on the Columbia,
Dwellers south on the banks of the Gila or Rio Grande —
    friendly gatherings, the characters and fun,
Dwellers up north in Minnesota and by the Yellowstone river —
    dwellers on coasts and off coasts,
Seal-fishers, whalers, arctic seamen breaking passages through
    the ice.

The shapes arise!
Shapes of factories, arsenals, foundries, markets;
Shapes of the two-threaded tracks of railroads;
Shapes of the sleepers of bridges, vast frameworks, girders,
    arches;
Shapes of the fleets of barges, towns, lake and canal craft,
    river craft.

The shapes arise!
Ship-yards and dry-docks along the Eastern and Western Seas,
    and in many a bay and by-place,
The live-oak kelsons, the pine planks, the spars, the
    hackmatack-roots for knees,
The ships themselves on their ways, the tiers of scaffolds, the
    workmen busy outside and inside,
The tools lying around, the great auger and little auger, the
    adze, bolt, line, square, gouge, and bead-plane.

10

The shapes arise!

The shape measur'd, saw'd, jack'd, join'd, stain'd,

The coffin-shape for the dead to lie within in his shroud;

The shape got out in posts, in the bedstead posts, in the posts
        of the bride's bed;

The shape of the little trough, the shape of the rockers
        beneath, the shape of the babe's cradle;

The shape of the floor-planks, the floor-planks for
        dancers' feet;

The shape of the planks of the family home, the home of the
        friendly parents and children,

The shape of the roof of the home of the happy young man
        and woman—the roof over the well-married young
        man and woman,

The roof over the supper joyously cook'd by the chaste wife,
        and joyously eaten by the chaste husband, content
        after his day's work.

The shapes arise!

The shape of the prisoner's place in the court-room, and of
        him or her seated in the place;

The shape of the liquor-bar lean'd against by the young rum-
        drinker and the old rum-drinker;

The shape of the shamed and angry stairs, trod by
        sneaking footsteps;

The shape of the sly settee, and the adulterous
        unwholesome couple;

The shape of the gambling-board with its devilish winnings
        and losings;

The shape of the step-ladder for the convicted and sentenced
        murderer, the murderer with haggard face and
        pinion'd arms,
The sheriff at hand with his deputies, the silent and white-
        lipp'd crowd, the dangling of the rope.

The shapes arise!
Shapes of doors giving many exits and entrances;
The door passing the dissever'd friend, flush'd and in haste;
The door that admits good news and bad news;
The door whence the son left home, confident and puff'd up;
The door he enter'd again from a long and scandalous
        absence, diseas'd, broken down, with out innocence,
        without means.

11

Her shape arises,
She, less guarded than ever, yet more guarded than ever;
The gross and soil'd she moves among do not make her gross
        and soil'd;
She knows the thoughts as she passes – nothing is conceal'd
        from her;
She is none the less considerate or friendly therefor;
She is the best belov'd – it is without exception – she has no
        reason to fear, and she does not fear;
Oaths, quarrels, hiccupp'd songs, smutty expressions, are idle
        to her as she passes;
She is silent – she is possess'd of herself – they do not
        offend her;
She receives them as the laws of nature receive them – she
        is strong,
She too is a law of nature – there is no law stronger than she is.

12

The main shapes arise!
Shapes of Democracy, total – result of centuries;
Shapes, ever projecting other shapes;
Shapes of turbulent manly cities;
Shapes of the friends and home-givers of the whole earth,
Shapes bracing the earth, and braced with the whole earth.

SONG OF THE OPEN ROAD

First published in 1856

1

AFOOT AND LIGHT-HEARTED, I take to the open road,
Healthy, free, the world before me,
The long brown path before me, leading wherever I choose.

Henceforth I ask not good-fortune – I myself am good fortune;
Henceforth I whimper no more, postpone no more,
        need nothing,
Strong and content, I travel the open road.

The earth – that is sufficient;
I do not want the constellations any nearer;
I know they are very well where they are;
I know they suffice for those who belong to them.

(Still here I carry my old delicious burdens;
I carry them, men and women – I carry them with me wherever
        I go;

I swear it is impossible for me to get rid of them;
I am fill'd with them, and I will fill them in return.)

2

You road I enter upon and look around! I believe you are not
        all that is here;
I believe that much unseen is also here.

Here the profound lesson of reception, neither preference
        or denial;
The black with his woolly head, the felon, the diseas'd, the
        illiterate person, are not denied;
The birth, the hasting after the physician, the beggar's tramp,
        the drunkard's stagger, the laughing party of
        mechanics,
The escaped youth, the rich person's carriage, the fop, the
        eloping couple,
The early market-man, the hearse, the moving of furniture into
        the town, the return back from the town,
They pass—I also pass—anything passes—none can be
        interdicted;
None but are accepted—none but are dear to me.

3

You air that serves me with breath to speak!
You objects that call from diffusion my meanings, and give
        them shape!
You light that wraps me and all things in delicate equable
        showers!
You paths worn in the irregular hollows by the roadsides!
I think you are latent with unseen existences—you are so dear
        to me.

You flagg'd walks of the cities! you strong curbs at the edges!
You ferries! you planks and posts of wharves! you timber-lined
        sides! you distant ships!
You rows of houses! you window-pierc'd facades! you roofs!
You porches and entrances! you copings and iron guards!
You windows whose transparent shells might expose so much!
You doors and ascending steps! you arches!
You gray stones of interminable pavements! you trodden
        crossings!
From all that has been near you, I believe you have imparted
        to yourselves, and now would impart the same secretly
        to me;
From the living and the dead I think you have peopled your
        impassive surfaces, and the spirits thereof would be
        evident and amicable with me.

4

The earth expanding right hand and left hand,
The picture alive, every part in its best light,
The music falling in where it is wanted, and stopping where it
        is not wanted,
The cheerful voice of the public road – the gay fresh sentiment
        of the road.

O highway I travel! O public road! do you say to me, *Do not
        leave me?*
Do you say, *Venture not? If you leave me, you are lost?*
Do you say, *I am already prepared – I am well-beaten and
        undenied – adhere to me?*

O public road! I say back, I am not afraid to leave you—yet I
      love you;
You express me better than I can express myself;
You shall be more to me than my poem.

I think heroic deeds were all conceiv'd in the open air, and all
      great poems also;
I think I could stop here myself, and do miracles;
(My judgments, thoughts, I henceforth try by the open air,
      the road;)
I think whatever I shall meet on the road I shall like, and
      whoever beholds me shall like me;
I think whoever I see must be happy.

5

From this hour, freedom!
From this hour I ordain myself loos'd of limits and
      imaginary lines,
Going where I list, my own master, total and absolute,
Listening to others, and considering well what they say,
Pausing, searching, receiving, contemplating,
Gently, but with undeniable will, divesting myself of the holds
      that would hold me.

I inhale great draughts of space;
The east and the west are mine, and the north and the south
      are mine.

I am larger, better than I thought;
I did not know I held so much goodness.

All seems beautiful to me;
I can repeat over to men and women, You have done such
  good to me, I would do the same to you.

I will recruit for myself and you as I go;
I will scatter myself among men and women as I go;
I will toss the new gladness and roughness among them;
Whoever denies me, it shall not trouble me;
Whoever accepts me, he or she shall be blessed, and shall
  bless me.

6

Now if a thousand perfect men were to appear, it would not
  amaze me;
Now if a thousand beautiful forms of women appear'd, it
  would not astonish me.

Now I see the secret of the making of the best persons,
It is to grow in the open air, and to eat and sleep with
  the earth.

Here a great personal deed has room;
A great deed seizes upon the hearts of the whole race of men,
Its effusion of strength and will overwhelms law, and mocks all
  authority and all argument against it.

Here is the test of wisdom;
Wisdom is not finally tested in schools;
Wisdom cannot be pass'd from one having it, to another not
  having it;

Wisdom is of the Soul, is not susceptible of proof, is its
          own proof,
Applies to all stages and objects and qualities, and is content,
Is the certainty of the reality and immortality of things, and
          the excellence of things;
Something there is in the float of the sight of things that
          provokes it out of the Soul.

Now I reexamine philosophies and religions,
They may prove well in lecture-rooms, yet not prove at all
          under the spacious clouds, and along the landscape
          and flowing currents.

Here is realization;
Here is a man tallied—he realizes here what he has in him;
The past, the future, majesty, love—if they are vacant of you,
          you are vacant of them.

Only the kernel of every object nourishes;
Where is he who tears off the husks for you and me?
Where is he that undoes stratagems and envelopes for you
          and me?

Here is adhesiveness—it is not previously fashion'd—it
          is apropos;
Do you know what it is, as you pass, to be loved by strangers?
Do you know the talk of those turning eye-balls?

7

Here is the efflux of the Soul;
The efflux of the Soul comes from within, through embower'd
          gates, ever provoking questions:

These yearnings, why are they? These thoughts in the
          darkness, why are they?
Why are there men and women that while they are nigh me,
          the sun-light expands my blood?
Why, when they leave me, do my pennants of joy sink flat
          and lank?
Why are there trees I never walk under, but large and
          melodious thoughts descend upon me?
(I think they hang there winter and summer on those trees,
          and always drop fruit as I pass;)
What is it I interchange so suddenly with strangers?
What with some driver, as I ride on the seat by his side?
What with some fisherman, drawing his seine by the shore, as
          I walk by, and pause?
What gives me to be free to a woman's or man's good-will?
          What gives them to be free to mine?

8

The efflux of the Soul is happiness—here is happiness;
I think it pervades the open air, waiting at all times;
Now it flows unto us—we are rightly charged.

Here rises the fluid and attaching character;
The fluid and attaching character is the freshness and
          sweetness of man and woman;
(The herbs of the morning sprout no fresher and sweeter every
          day out of the roots of themselves, than it sprouts
          fresh and sweet continually out of itself.)

Toward the fluid and attaching character exudes the sweat of
          the love of young and old;

From it falls distill'd the charm that mocks beauty and
      attainments;
Toward it heaves the shuddering longing ache of contact.

9

Allons! whoever you are, come travel with me!
Traveling with me, you find what never tires.

The earth never tires;
The earth is rude, silent, incomprehensible at first—Nature
      is rude and incomprehensible at first;
Be not discouraged—keep on—there are divine things,
      well envelop'd;
I swear to you there are divine things more beautiful than
      words can tell.

Allons! we must not stop here!
However sweet these laid-up stores—however convenient this
      dwelling, we cannot remain here;
However shelter'd this port, and however calm these waters, we
      must not anchor here;
However welcome the hospitality that surrounds us, we are
      permitted to receive it but a little while.

10

Allons! the inducements shall be greater;
We will sail pathless and wild seas;
We will go where winds blow, waves dash, and the Yankee
      clipper speeds by under full sail.

Allons! with power, liberty, the earth, the elements!
Health, defiance, gayety, self-esteem, curiosity;
Allons! from all formules!
From your formules, O bat-eyed and materialistic priests!

The stale cadaver blocks up the passage – the burial waits
        no longer.

Allons! yet take warning!
He traveling with me needs the best blood, thews, endurance;
None may come to the trial, till he or she bring courage
        and health.

Come not here if you have already spent the best of yourself;
Only those may come, who come in sweet and determin'd bodies;
No diseas'd person – no rum-drinker or venereal taint is
        permitted here.

I and mine do not convince by arguments, similes, rhymes;
We convince by our presence.

11

Listen! I will be honest with you;
I do not offer the old smooth prizes, but offer rough
        new prizes;
These are the days that must happen to you:

You shall not heap up what is call'd riches,
You shall scatter with lavish hand all that you earn or achieve,
You but arrive at the city to which you were destin'd – you
        hardly settle yourself to satisfaction, before you are
        call'd by an irresistible call to depart,

You shall be treated to the ironical smiles and mockings of
            those who remain behind you;
What beckonings of love you receive, you shall only answer
            with passionate kisses of parting,
You shall not allow the hold of those who spread their reach'd
            hands toward you.

12

Allons! after the GREAT COMPANIONS! and to belong
            to them!
They too are on the road! they are the swift and majestic men!
            they are the greatest women.

Over that which hinder'd them – over that which retarded –
            passing impediments large or small,
Committers of crimes, committers of many beautiful virtues,
Enjoyers of calms of seas, and storms of seas,
Sailors of many a ship, walkers of many a mile of land,
Habitués of many distant countries, habitués of far-distant
            dwellings,
Trusters of men and women, observers of cities, solitary toilers,
Pausers and contemplators of tufts, blossoms, shells of
            the shore,
Dancers at wedding-dances, kissers of brides, tender helpers of
            children, bearers of children,
Soldiers of revolts, standers by gaping graves, lowerers down
            of coffins,
Journeyers over consecutive seasons, over the years – the
            curious years, each emerging from that which
            preceded it,

Journeyers as with companions, namely, their own
       diverse phases,
Forth-steppers from the latent unrealized baby-days,
Journeyers gayly with their own youth – Journeyers with their
       bearded and well-grain'd manhood,
Journeyers with their womanhood, ample, unsurpass'd,
       content,
Journeyers with their own sublime old age of manhood
       or womanhood,
Old age, calm, expanded, broad with the haughty breadth of
       the universe,
Old age, flowing free with the delicious near-by freedom
       of death.

13

Allons! to that which is endless, as it was beginningless,
To undergo much, tramps of days, rests of nights,
To merge all in the travel they tend to, and the days and nights
       they tend do,
Again to merge them in the start of superior journeys;
To see nothing anywhere but what you may reach it and
       pass it,
To conceive no time, however distant, but what you may reach
       it and pass it,
To look up or down no road but it stretches and waits for
       you – however long, but it stretches and waits for you;
To see no being, not God's or any, but you also go thither,
To see no possession but you may possess it – enjoying all
       without labor or purchase – abstracting the feast, yet
       not abstracting one particle of it;

To take the best of the farmer's farm and the rich man's elegant
          villa, and the chaste blessings of the well-married
          couple, and the fruits of orchards and flowers
          of gardens,
To take to your use out of the compact cities as you
          pass through,
To carry buildings and streets with you afterward wherever
          you go,
To gather the minds of men out of their brains as you
          encounter them – to gather the love out of their hearts,
To take your lovers on the road with you, for all that you leave
          them behind you,
To know the universe itself as a road – as many roads – as roads
          for traveling souls.

14

The Soul travels;
The body does not travel as much as the soul;
The body has just as great a work as the soul, and parts away
          at last for the journeys of the soul.

All parts away for the progress of souls;
All religion, all solid things, arts, governments, – all that was or
          is apparent upon this globe or any globe, falls into
          niches and corners before the procession of Souls
          along the grand roads of the universe.

Of the progress of the souls of men and women along the
          grand roads of the universe, all other progress is the
          needed emblem and sustenance.

Forever alive, forever forward,
Stately, solemn, sad, withdrawn, baffled, mad, turbulent,
          feeble, dissatisfied,
Desperate, proud, fond, sick, accepted by men, rejected
          by men,
They go! they go! I know that they go, but I know not where
          they go;
But I know that they go toward the best—toward something great.

15

Allons! whoever you are! come forth!
You must not stay sleeping and dallying there in the house,
          though you built it, or though it has been built for you.
Allons! out of the dark confinement!
It is useless to protest—I know all, and expose it.

Behold, through you as bad as the rest,
Through the laughter, dancing, dining, supping, of people,
Inside of dresses and ornaments, inside of those wash'd and
          trimm'd faces,
Behold a secret silent loathing and despair.

No husband, no wife, no friend, trusted to hear the confession;
Another self, a duplicate of every one, skulking and hiding
          it goes,
Formless and wordless through the streets of the cities, polite
          and bland in the parlors,
In the cars of rail-roads, in steamboats, in the public assembly,

Home to the houses of men and women, at the table, in the
          bed-room, everywhere,
Smartly attired, countenance smiling, form upright, death
          under the breast-bones, hell under the skull-bones,
Under the broadcloth and gloves, under the ribbons and
          artificial flowers,
Keeping fair with the customs, speaking not a syllable of itself,
Speaking of anything else, but never of itself.

16

Allons! through struggles and wars!
The goal that was named cannot be countermanded.

Have the past struggles succeeded?
What has succeeded? yourself? your nation? nature?
Now understand me well—It is provided in the essence of
          things, that from any fruition of success, no matter
          what, shall come forth something to make a greater
          struggle necessary.

My call is the call of battle—I nourish active rebellion;
He going with me must go well arm'd;
He going with me goes often with spare diet, poverty, angry
          enemies, desertions.

17

Allons! the road is before us!
It is safe—I have tried it—my own feet have tried it well.

Allons! be not detain'd!
Let the paper remain on the desk unwritten, and the book on
          the shelf unopen'd!

Let the tools remain in the workshop! let the money
      remain unearn'd!
Let the school stand! mind not the cry of the teacher!
Let the preacher preach in his pulpit! let the lawyer plead in
      the court, and the judge expound the law.

Mon enfant! I give you my hand!
I give you my love, more precious than money,
I give you myself, before preaching or law;
Will you give me yourself? will you come travel with me?
Shall we stick by each other as long as we live?

As I Lay with My Head in Your Lap, Camerado

As I lay with my head in your lap, Camerado,
The confession I made I resume—what I said to you in the
      open air I resume:
I know I am restless, and make others so;
I know my words are weapons, full of danger, full of death;
(Indeed I am myself the real soldier;
It is not he, there, with his bayonet, and not the red-striped
      artilleryman;)
For I confront peace, security, and all the settled laws, to
      unsettle them;
I am more resolute because all have denied me, than I could
      ever have been had all accepted me;
I heed not, and have never heeded, either experience, cautions,
      majorities, nor ridicule;

And the threat of what is call'd hell is little or nothing to me;
And the lure of what is call'd heaven is little or nothing to me;
. . . Dear camerado! I confess I have urged you onward with
      me, and still urge you, without the least idea what is
      our destination,
Or whether we shall be victorious, or utterly quell'd
      and defeated.

CROSSING BROOKLYN FERRY

First published in 1856 under title of "Sun-Down Poem"

1

FLOOD-TIDE BELOW ME! I watch you face to face;
Clouds of the west! sun there half an hour high! I see you also
      face to face.

Crowds of men and women attired in the usual costumes! how
      curious you are to me!
On the ferry-boats, the hundreds and hundreds that cross,
      returning home, are more curious to me than
      you suppose;
And you that shall cross from shore to shore years hence, are
      more to me, and more in my meditations, than you
      might suppose.

2

The impalpable sustenance of me from all things, at all hours
      of the day;
The simple, compact, well-join'd scheme—myself disintegrated,
      every one disintegrated, yet part of the scheme;

The similitudes of the past, and those of the future;
The glories strung like beads on my smallest sights and
          hearings – on the walk in the street, and the passage
          over the river;
The current rushing so swiftly, and swimming with me
          far away;
The others that are to follow me, the ties between me
          and them;
The certainty of others – the life, love, sight, hearing of others.

Others will enter the gates of the ferry, and cross from
          shore to shore;
Others will watch the run of the flood-tide;
Others will see the shipping of Manhattan north and west, and
          the heights of Brooklyn to the south and east;
Others will see the islands large and small;
Fifty years hence, others will see them as they cross, the sun
          half an hour high;
A hundred years hence, or ever so many hundred years hence,
          others will see them,
Will enjoy the sunset, the pouring in of the flood-tide, the
          falling back to the sea of the ebb-tide.

3

It avails not, neither time or place – distance avails not;
I am with you, you men and women of a generation, or ever so
          many generations hence;
I project myself – also I return – I am with you, and know
          how it is.

Just as you feel when you look on the river and sky, so I felt;
Just as any of you is one of a living crowd, I was one of
      a crowd;
Just as you are refresh'd by the gladness of the river and the
      bright flow, I was refresh'd;
Just as you stand and lean on the rail, yet hurry with the swift
      current, I stood, yet was hurried;]
Just as you look on the numberless masts of ships, and the
      thick-stem'd pipes of steamboats, I look'd.

I too may and many a time cross'd the river, the sun half an
      hour high;
I watched the Twelfth-month sea-gulls—I saw them high in
      the air, floating with motionless wings, oscillating
      their bodies,
I saw how the glistening yellow lit up parts of their bodies, and
      left the rest in strong shadow,
I saw the slow-wheeling circles, and the gradual edging toward
      the south.

I too saw the reflection of the summer sky in the water,
Had my eyes dazzled by the shimmering track of beams,
Look'd at the fine centrifugal spokes of light around the shape
      of my head in the sun-lit water,
Look'd on the haze on the hills southward and southwestward,
Look'd on the vapor as it flew in fleeces tinged with violet,
Look'd toward the lower bay to notice the arriving ships,
Saw their approach, saw aboard those that were near me,
Saw the white sails of schooners and sloops—saw the ships
      at anchor,
The sailors at work in the rigging, or out astride the spars,

The round masts, the swinging motion of the hulls, the slender
      serpentine pennants,
The large and small steamers in motion, the pilots in their
      pilot-houses,
The white wake left by the passage, the quick tremulous whirl
      of the wheels,
The flags of all nations, the falling of them at sun-set,
The scallop-edged waves in the twilight, the ladled cups, the
      frolicsome crests and glistening,
The stretch afar growing dimmer and dimmer, the gray walls of
      the granite store-houses by the docks,
On the river the shadowy group, the big steam-tug closely
      flank'd on each side by the barges – the hay-boat, the
      belated lighter,
On the neighboring shore, the fires from the foundry
      chimneys burning high and glaringly into the night,
Casting their flicker of black, contrasted with wild red and
      yellow light, over the tops of houses, and down into
      the clefts of streets.

4

These, and all else, were to me the same as they are to you;
I project myself a moment to tell you – also I return.

I loved well those cities;
I loved well the stately and rapid river;
The men and women I saw were all near to me;
Others the same – others who look back on me, because I
      look'd forward to them;
(The time will come, though I stop here to-day and to-night.)

5

What is it, then, between us?
What is the count of the scores or hundreds of years
    between us?

Whatever it is, it avails not—distance avails not, and place
    avails not.

6

I too lived—Brooklyn, of ample hills, was mine;
I too walk'd the streets of Manhattan Island, and bathed in the
    waters around it;
I too felt the curious abrupt questionings stir within me,
In the day, among crowds of people, sometimes they came
    upon me,
In my walks home late at night, or as I lay in my bed, they
    came upon me.

I too had been struck from the float forever held in solution;
I too had receiv'd identity by my Body;
That I was, I knew was of my body—and what I should be, I
    knew I should be of my body.

7

It is not upon you alone the dark patches fall,
The dark threw patches down upon me also;
The best I had done seem'd to me blank and suspicious;
My great thoughts, as I supposed them, were they not in reality
    meagre? would not people laugh at me?

It is not you alone who know what it is to be evil;
I am he who knew what it was to be evil;
I too knitted the old knot of contrariety,
Blabb'd, blush'd, resented, lied, stole, grudg'd,
Had guile, anger, lust, hot wishes I dared not speak,
Was wayward, vain, greedy, shallow, sly, cowardly, malignant;
The wolf, the snake, the hog, not wanting in me,
The cheating look, the frivolous word, the adulterous wish,
        not wanting,
Refusals, hates, postponements, meanness, laziness, none of
        these wanting.

8

But I was Manhattanese, friendly and proud!
I was call'd by my nighest name by clear loud voices of young
        men as they saw me approaching or passing,
Felt their arms on my neck as I stood, or the negligent leaning
        of their flesh against me as I sat,
Saw many I loved in the street, or ferry-boat, or public
        assembly, yet never told them a word,
Lived the same life with the rest, the same old laughing,
        gnawing, sleeping,
Play'd the part that still looks back on the actor or actress,
The same old role, the role that is what we make it, as great as
        we like,
Or as small as we like, or both great and small.

9

Closer yet I approach you;
What thought you have of me, I had as much of you—I laid in
        my stores in advance;
I consider'd long and seriously of you before you were born.

Who was to know what should come home to me?
Who knows but I am enjoying this?
Who knows but I am as good as looking at you now, for all
          you cannot see me?

It is not you alone, nor I alone;
Not a few races, nor a few generations, nor a few centuries;
It is that each came, or comes, or shall come, from its
          due emission,
From the general centre of all, and forming a part of all:
Everything indicates – the smallest does, and the largest does;
A necessary film envelopes all, and envelopes the Soul for a
          proper time.

                              10

Now I am curious what sight can ever be more stately and
          admirable to me than my mast-hemm'd Manhattan,
My river and sun-set, and my scallop-edg'd waves of flood-tide,
The sea-gulls oscillating their bodies, the hay-boat in the
          twilight, and the belated lighter;
Curious what Gods can exceed these that clasp me by the
          hand, and with voices I love call me promptly and
          loudly by my nighest name as I approach;
Curious what is more subtle than this which ties me to the
          woman or man that looks in my face,
Which fuses me into you now, and pours my meaning
          into you.

We understand, then, do we not?
What I promis'd without mentioning it, have you not
          accepted?

What the study could not teach—what the preaching could not
      accomplish, is accomplish'd, is it not?
What the push of reading could not start, is started by me
      personally, is it not?

11

Flow on, river! flow with the flood-tide, and ebb with
      the ebb-tide!
Frolic on, crested and scallop-edg'd waves!
Gorgeous clouds of the sun-set! drench with your splendor
      me, or the men and women generations after me;
Cross from shore to shore, countless crowds of passengers!
Stand up, tall masts of Mannahatta!—stand up, beautiful hills
      of Brooklyn!
Throb, baffled and curious brain! throw out questions
      and answers!
Suspend here and everywhere, eternal float of solution!
Gaze, loving and thirsting eyes, in the house, or street, or
      public assembly!
Sound out, voices of young men! loudly and musically call me
      by my nighest name!
Live, old life! play the part that looks back on the actor
      or actress!
Play the old role, the role that is great or small, according as
      one makes it!
Consider, you who peruse me, whether I may not in unknown
      ways be looking upon you;
Be firm, rail over the river, to support those who lean idly, yet
      haste with the hasting current;
Fly on, sea-birds! fly sideways, or wheel in large circles high in
      the air;

Receive the summer sky, you water! and faithfully hold it, till
        all downcast eyes have time to take it from you;
Diverge, fine spokes of light, from the shape of my head, or
        any one's head, in the sun-lit water;
Come on, ships from the lower bay! pass up or down, white-
        sail'd schooners, sloops, lighters!
Flaunt away, flags of all nations! be duly lower'd at sunset;
Burn high your fires, foundry chimneys! cast black shadows at
        nightfall! cast red and yellow light over the tops of
        the houses;
Appearances, now or henceforth, indicate what you are;
You necessary film, continue to envelop the soul;
About my body for me, and your body for you, be hung our
        divinest aromas;
Thrive, cities! bring your freight, bring your shows, ample and
        sufficient rivers;
Expand, being than which none else is perhaps more spiritual;
Keep your places, objects than which none else is more
        lasting.

12

We descend upon you and all things—we arrest you all;
We realize the soul only by you, you faithful solids and fluids;
Through you color, form, location, sublimity, ideality;
Through you every proof, comparison, and all the suggestions
        and determinations of ourselves.

You have waited, you always wait, you dumb, beautiful
        ministers! you novices!
We receive you with free sense at last, and are insatiate
        hence-forward;

Not you any more shall be able to foil us, or withhold
          yourselves from us;
We use you, and do not cast you aside—we plant you
          permanently within us;
We fathom you not—we love you—there is perfection
          in you also;
You furnish your parts toward eternity;
Great or small, you furnish your parts toward the soul.

NOW LIST TO MY MORNING'S ROMANZA
First published in 1855

1

Now LIST TO my morning's romanza—I tell the signs of
          the Answerer;
To the cities and farms I sing, as they spread in the sunshine
          before me.

A young man comes to me bearing a message from
          his brother;
How shall the young man know the whether and when
          of his brother?
Tell him to send me the signs.

And I stand before the young man face to face, and take his
      right hand in my left hand, and his left hand in my
      right hand,
And I answer for his brother, and for men, and I answer for
      him that answers for all, and send these signs.

2

Him all wait for—him all yield up to—his word is decisive
      and final,
Him they accept, in him lave, in him perceive themselves, as
      amid light,
Him they immerse, and he immerses them.

Beautiful women, the haughtiest nations, laws, the landscape,
      people, animals,
The profound earth and its attributes, and the unquiet ocean,
      (so tell I my morning's romanza;)
All enjoyments and properties, and money, and whatever
      money will buy,
The best farms—others toiling and planting, and he
      unavoidably reaps,
The noblest and costliest cities—others grading and building,
      and he domiciles there;
Nothing for any one, but what is for him—near and far are for
      him, the ships in the offing,
The perpetual shows and marches on land, are for him, if they
      are for any body.

He puts things in their attitudes;
He puts to-day out of himself, with plasticity and love;

He places his own city, times, reminiscences, parents, brothers
       and sisters, associations, employment, politics, so that
       the rest never shame them afterward, nor assume to
       command them.

He is the answerer;
What can be answer'd he answers – and what cannot be
       answer'd, he shows how it cannot be answer'd.

3

A man is a summons and challenge;
(It is vain to skulk – Do you hear that mocking and laughter?
       Do you hear the ironical echoes?)

Books, friendships, philosophers, priests, action, pleasure,
       pride, beat up and down, seeking to give satisfaction;
He indicates the satisfaction, and indicates them that beat up
       and down also.

Whichever the sex, whatever the season or place, he may go
       freshly and gently and safely, by day or by night;
He has the pass-key of hearts – to him the response of the
       prying of hands on the knobs.

His welcome is universal – the flow of beauty is not more
       welcome or universal than he is;
The person he favors by day, or sleeps with at night, is blessed.

4

Every existence has its idiom – everything has an idiom
       and tongue;

He resolves all tongues into his own, and bestows it upon
      men, and any man translates, and any man translates
      himself also;
One part does not counteract another part—he is the joiner—
      he sees how they join.

He says indifferently and alike, *How are you, friend?* to the
      President at his levee,
And he says, *Good-day, my brother!* to Cudge that hoes in the
      sugar-field,
And both understand him, and know that his speech is right.

He walks with perfect ease in the Capitol,
He walks among the Congress, and one Representative says to
      another, *Here is our equal, appearing and new.*

Then the mechanics take him for a mechanic,
And the soldiers suppose him to be a soldier, and the sailors
      that he has follow'd the sea,
And the authors take him for an author, and the artists for
      an artist,
And the laborers perceive he could labor with them and
      love them;
No matter what the work is, that he is the one to follow it, or
      has follow'd it,
No matter what the nation, that he might find his brothers and
      sisters there.

The English believe he comes of their English stock,
A Jew to the Jew he seems—a Russ to the Russ—usual and near,
      removed from none.

Whoever he looks at in the traveler's coffee-house claims him,
The Italian or Frenchman is sure, and the German is sure, and
      the Spaniard is sure, and the island Cuban is sure;
The engineer, the deck-hand on the great lakes, or on the
      Mississippi, or St. Lawrence, or Sacramento, or
      Hudson, or Paumanok Sound, claims him.

The gentleman of perfect blood acknowledges his perfect blood;
The insulter, the prostitute, the angry person, the beggar, see
      themselves in the ways of him—he strangely
      transmutes them,
They are not vile any more—they hardly know themselves,
      they are so grown.

I HEAR AMERICA SINGING

First published in 1860 where line 1 reads "American Mouth-Songs"

I HEAR AMERICA singing, the varied carols I hear;
Those of mechanics—each one singing his, as it should be,
      blithe and strong;
The carpenter singing his, as he measures his plank or beam,
The mason singing his, as he makes ready for work, or leaves
      off work;
The boatman singing what belongs to him in his boat—the
      deckhand singing on the steamboat deck;
The shoemaker singing as he sits on his bench—the hatter
      singing as he stands;

The wood-cutter's song—the ploughboy's, on his way in the
            morning, or at the noon intermission, or at sundown;
The delicious singing of the mother—or of the young wife at
            work—or of the girl sewing or washing—Each singing
            what belongs to her, and to none else;
The day what belongs to the day—At night, the party of young
            fellows, robust, friendly,
Singing, with open mouths, their strong melodious songs.

CAROL OF OCCUPATIONS

First published in 1855

1

COME CLOSER TO me;
Push close, my lovers, and take the best I possess;
Yield closer and closer, and give me the best you possess.

This is unfinish'd business with me—How is it with you?
(I was chill'd with the cold types, cylinder, wet paper
            between us.)

Male and Female!
I pass so poorly with paper and types, I must pass with the
            contact of bodies and souls.

American masses!
I do not thank you for liking me as I am, and liking the touch
            of me—I know that it is good for you to do so.

2

This is the carol of occupations;
In the labor of engines and trades, and the labor of fields,
        I find the developments,
And find the eternal meanings.

Workmen and Workwomen!
Were all educations, practical and ornamental, well display'd
        out of me, what would it amount to?
Were I as the head teacher, charitable proprietor, wise
        statesman, what would it amount to?
Were I to you as the boss employing and paying you, would
        that satisfy you?

The learn'd, virtuous, benevolent, and the usual terms;
A man like me, and never the usual terms.

Neither a servant nor a master am I;
I take no sooner a large price than a small price—I will have
        my own, whoever enjoys me;
I will be even with you, and you shall be even with me.

If you stand at work in a shop, I stand as nigh as the nighest in
        the same shop;
If you bestow gifts on your brother or dearest friend, I demand
        as good as your brother or dearest friend;
If your lover, husband, wife, is welcome by day or night, I must
        be personally as welcome;
If you become degraded, criminal, ill, then I become so for
        your sake;

If you remember your foolish and outlaw'd deeds, do you
          think I cannot remember my own foolish and outlaw'd
          deeds?
If you carouse at the table, I carouse at the opposite side
          of the table;
If you meet some stranger in the streets, and love him or
          her—why I often meet strangers in the street, and love
          them.

Why, what have you thought of yourself?
Is it you then that thought yourself less?
Is it you that thought the President greater than you?
Or the rich better off than you? or the educated wiser
          than you?

Because your are greasy or pimpled, or that you were once
          drunk, or a thief,
Or diseas'd, or rheumatic, or a prostitute—or are so now;
Or from frivolity or impotence, or that you are no scholar, and
          never saw your name in print,
Do you give in that you are any less immortal?

3

Souls of men and women! it is not you I call unseen, unheard,
          untouchable and untouching;
It is not you I go argue pro and con about, and to settle
          whether you are alive or no;
I own publicly who you are, if nobody else owns.

Grown, half-grown, and babe, of this country and every
        country, in-doors and out-doors, one just as much as
        the other, I see,
And all else behind or through them.

The wife–and she is not one jot less than the husband;
The daughter–and she is just as good as the son;
The mother–and she is every bit as much as the father.

Offspring of ignorant and poor, boys apprenticed to trades,
Young fellows working on farms, and old fellows working
        on farms,
Sailor-men, merchant-men, coasters, immigrants,
All these I see–but nigher and farther the same I see;
None shall escape me, and none shall wish to escape me.

I bring what you much need, yet always have,
Not money, amours, dress, eating, but as good;
I send no agent or medium, offer no representative of value,
        but offer the value itself.

There is something that comes home to one now
        and perpetually;
It is not what is printed, preach'd, discussed–it eludes
        discussion and print;
It is not to be put in a book–it is not in this book;
It is for you, whoever you are–it is no farther from you than
        your hearing and sight are from you;
It is hinted by nearest, commonest, readiest–it is ever
        provoked by them.

You may read in many languages, yet read nothing about it;
You may read the President's Message, and read nothing about
     it there;
Nothing in the reports from the State department or Treasury
     department, or in the daily papers or the weekly papers,
Or in the census or revenue returns, prices current, or any
     accounts of stock.

4

The sun and stars that float in the open air;
The apple-shaped earth, and we upon it—surely the drift of
     them is something grand!
I do not know what it is, except that it is grand, and that
     it is happiness,
And that the enclosing purport of us here is not a speculation,
     or bon-mot, or reconnoissance,
And that it is not something which by luck may turn out well
     for us, and without luck must be a failure for us,
And not something which may yet be retracted in a
     certain contingency.

The light and shade, the curious sense of body and identity,
     the greed that with perfect complaisance devours all
     things, the endless pride and out-stretching of man,
     unspeakable joys and sorrows,
The wonder every one sees in every one else he sees, and the
     wonders that fill each minute of time forever,
Have you reckon'd them for, camerado?
Have you reckon'd them for a trade, or farm-work? or for the
     profits of a store?

Or to achieve yourself a position? or to fill a gentleman's
	leisure, or a lady's leisure?

Have you reckon'd the landscape took substance and form that
	it might be painted in a picture?
Or men and women that they might be written of, and
	songs sung?
Or the attraction of gravity, and the great laws and harmonious
	combinations, and the fluids of the air, as subjects for
	the savans?
Or the brown land and the blue sea for maps and charts?
Or the stars to be put in constellations and named
	fancy names?
Or that the growth of seeds is for agricultural tables, or
	agriculture itself?

Old institutions – these arts, libraries, legends, collections, and
	the practice handed along in manufactures – will we
	rate them so high?
Will we rate our cash and business high? – I have no objection;
I rate them as high as the highest – then a child born of a
	woman and man I rate beyond all rate.

We thought our Union grand, and our Constitution grand;
I do not say they are not grand and good, for they are;
I am this day just as much in love with them as you;
Then I am in love with you, and with all my fellows upon
	the earth.

We consider bibles and religions divine – I do not say they are
	not divine;

I say they have all grown out of you, and may grow out of
        you still;
It is not they who give the life—it is you who give the life;
Leaves are not more shed from the trees, or trees from the
        earth, than they are shed out of you.

5

When the psalm sings instead of the singer;
When the script preaches instead of the preacher;
When the pulpit descends and goes, instead of the carver that
        carved the supporting desk;
When I can touch the body of books, by night or by day, and
        when they touch my body back again;
When a university course convinces, like a slumbering woman
        and child convince;
When the minted gold in the vault smiles like the night-
        watchman's daughter;
When warrantee deeds loafe in chairs opposite, and are my
        friendly companions;
I intend to reach them my hand, and make as much of them
        as I do of men and women like you.

The sum of all known reverence I add up in you, whoever
        you are;
The President is there in the White House for you—it is not
        you who are here for him;
The Secretaries act in their bureaus for you—not you here
        for them;
The Congress convenes every Twelfth-month for you;
Laws, courts, the forming of States, the charters of cities,
        the going and coming of commerce and mails,
        are all for you.

List close, my scholars dear!
All doctrines, all politics and civilization, exurge from you;
All sculpture and monuments, and anything inscribed
        anywhere, are tallied in you;
The gist of histories and statistics as far back as the records
        reach, is in you this hour, and myths and tales
        the same;
If you were not breathing and walking here, where would they
        all be?
The most renown'd poems would be ashes, orations and plays
        would be vacuums.

All architecture is what you do to it when you look upon it;
(Did you think it was in the white or gray stone? or the lines
        of the arches and cornices?)

All music is what awakes from you when you are reminded by
        the instruments;
It is not the violins and the cornets – it is not the oboe nor the
        beating drums, nor the score of the baritone singer
        singing his sweet romanza – nor that of the men's
        chorus, nor that of the women's chorus,
It is nearer and farther than they.

6

Will the whole come back then?
Can each see signs of the best by a look in the looking-glass?
        is there nothing greater or more?
Does all sit there with you, with the mystic, unseen Soul?

Strange and hard that paradox true I give;
Objects gross and the unseen Soul are one.

House-building, measuring, sawing the boards;
Blacksmithing, glass-blowing, nail-making, coopering, tin-
      roofing, shingle-dressing,
Ship-joining, dock-building, fish-curing, ferrying, flagging of
      side-walks by flaggers,
The pump, the pile-driver, the great derrick, the coal-kiln and
      brick-kiln,
Coal-mines, and all that is down there,—the lamps in the
      darkness, echoes, songs, what meditations, what vast
      native thoughts looking through smutch'd faces,
Iron-works, forge-fires in the mountains, or by the river-
      banks—men around feeling the melt with huge
      crowbars—lumps of ore, the due combining of ore,
      limestone, coal—the blast-furnace and the puddling-
      furnace, the loup-lump at the bottom of the melt at
      last—the rolling-mill, the stumpy bars of pig-iron, the
      strong, clean-shaped T-rail for railroads;
Oil-works, silk-works, white-lead-works, the sugar-house,
      steam-saws, the great mills and factories;
Stone-cutting, shapely trimmings for façades, or window or
      door-lintels—the mallet, the tooth-chisel, the jib to
      protect the thumb,
Oakum, the oakum-chisel, the caulking-iron—the kettle of
      boiling vault-cement, and the fire under the kettle,
The cotton-bale, the stevedore's hook, the saw and buck of the
      sawyer, the mould of the moulder, the working-knife of
      the butcher, the ice-saw, and all the work with ice,
The implements for daguerreotyping—the tools of the rigger,
      grappler, sail-maker, block-maker,
Goods of gutta-percha, papier-maché, colors, brushes, brush-
      making, glazier's implements,

The veneer and glue-pot, the confectioner's ornaments, the
        decanter and glasses, the shears and flat-iron,
The awl and knee-strap, the pint measure and quart measure,
        the counter and stool, the writing-pen of quill or
        metal – the making of all sorts of edged tools,
The brewery, brewing, the malt, the vats, every thing that
        is done by brewers, also by wine-makers, also
        vinegar-makers,
Leather-dressing, coach-making, boiler-making, rope-twisting,
        distilling, sign-painting, lime-burning, cotton-
        picking – electro-plating, electrotyping, stereotyping,
Stave-machines, planing-machines, reaping-machines,
        ploughing-machines, thrashing-machines, steam
        wagons,
The cart of the carman, the omnibus, the ponderous dray;
Pyrotechny, letting off color'd fire-works at night, fancy figures
        and jets;
Beef on the butcher's stall, the slaughter-house of the butcher,
        the butcher in his killing-clothes,
The pens of live pork, the killing-hammer, the hog-hook, the
        scalder's tub, gutting, the cutter's cleaver, the packer's
        maul, and the plenteous winter-work of pork-packing;
Flour-works, grinding of wheat, rye, maize, rice – the barrels
        and the half and quarter barrels, the loaded barges, the
        high piles on wharves and levees;
The men, and the work of the men, on railroads, coasters, fish-
        boats, canals;
The daily routine of your own or any man's life – the shop,
        yard, store, or factory;
These shows all near you by day and night – workman!
        whoever you are, your daily life!

In that and them the heft of the heaviest—in them far more
            than you estimated, and far less also;
In them realities for you and me—in them poems for you
            and me;
In them, not yourself—you and your Soul enclose all things,
            regardless of estimation;
In them the development good—in them, all themes and hints.

I do not affirm what you see beyond is futile—I do not advise
            you to stop;
I do not say leadings you thought great are not great;
But I say that none lead to greater, than those lead to.

7

Will you seek afar off? you surely come back at last,
In things best known to you, finding the best, or as good as
            the best,
In folks nearest to you finding the sweetest, strongest,
            lovingest;
Happiness, knowledge, not in another place, but in this
            place—not for another hour, but this hour:
Man in the first you see or touch—always in friend, brother,
            nighest neighbor—Woman in mother, lover, wife;
The popular tastes and employments taking precedence in
            poems or any where,
You workwomen and workmen of These States having your
            own divine and strong life,
And all else giving place to men and women like you.

THE SLEEPERS

First published in 1855

1

I WANDER ALL night in my vision,
Stepping with light feet, swiftly and noiselessly stepping
          and stopping,
Bending with open eyes over the shut eyes of sleepers,
Wandering and confused, lost to myself, ill-assorted,
          contradictory,
Pausing, gazing, bending, and stopping.

How solemn they look there, stretch'd and still!
How quiet they breathe, the little children in their cradles!

The wretched features of ennuyés, the white features of
          corpses, the livid faces of drunkards, the sick-gray
          faces of onanists,
The gash'd bodies on battle-fields, the insane in their strong-
          door'd rooms, the sacred idiots, the new-born emerging
          from gates, and the dying emerging from gates,
The night pervades them and unfolds them.

The married couple sleep calmly in their bed—he with his
          palm on the hip of the wife, and she with her palm on
          the hip of the husband,
The sisters sleep lovingly side by side in their bed,
The men sleep lovingly side by side in theirs,
And the mother sleeps, with her little child carefully wrapt.

The blind sleep, and the deaf and dumb sleep,
The prisoner sleeps well in the prison – the run-away
son sleeps;
The murderer that is to be hung next day – how does he sleep?
And the murder'd person – how does he sleep?

The female that loves unrequited sleeps,
And the male that loves unrequited sleeps,
The head of the money-maker that plotted all day sleeps,
And the enraged and treacherous dispositions – all, all sleep.

2

I stand in the dark with drooping eyes by the worst-suffering
and the most restless,
I pass my hands soothingly to and fro a few inches from them,
The restless sink in their beds – they fitfully sleep.

Now I pierce the darkness – new beings appear,
The earth recedes from me into the night,
I saw that it was beautiful, and I see that what is not the earth
is beautiful.

I go from bedside to bedside – I sleep close with the other
sleepers, each in turn,
I dream in my dream all the dreams of the other dreamers,
And I become the other dreamers.

3

I am a dance – Play up, there! the fit is whirling me fast!

I am the ever-laughing–it is new moon and twilight,
I see the hiding of douceurs–I see nimble ghosts whichever
      way I look,
Cache, and cache again, deep in the ground and sea, and
      where it is neither ground or sea.

Well do they do their jobs, those journeymen divine,
Only from me can they hide nothing, and would not if
      they could,
I reckon I am their boss, and they make me a pet besides,
And surround me and lead me, and run ahead when I walk,
To lift their cunning covers, to signify me with stretch'd arms,
      and resume the way;
Onward we move! a gay gang of blackguards! with mirth-
      shouting music, and wild-flapping pennants of joy!

4

I am the actor, the actress, the voter, the politician;
The emigrant and the exile, the criminal that stood in the box,
He who has been famous, and he who shall be famous
      after to-day,
The stammerer, the well-form'd person, the wasted or
      feeble person.

5

I am she who adorn'd herself and folded her hair expectantly,
My truant lover has come, and it is dark.

Double yourself and receive me, darkness!
Receive me and my lover too–he will not let me go
      without him.

I roll myself upon you, as upon a bed – I resign myself
    to the dusk.

6

He whom I call answers me, and takes the place of my lover,
He rises with me silently from the bed.

Darkness! you are gentler than my lover – his flesh was sweaty
    and panting,
I feel the hot moisture yet that he left me.

My hands are spread forth, I pass them in all directions,
I would sound up the shadowy shore to which you
    are journeying.

Be careful, darkness! already, what was it touch'd me?
I thought my lover had gone, else darkness and he are one,
I hear the heart-beat – I follow, I fade away.

7

O hot-cheek'd and blushing! O foolish hectic!
O for pity's sake, no one must see me now! my clothes were
    stolen while I was abed,
Now I am thrust forth, where shall I run?

Pier that I saw dimly last night, when I look'd from
    the windows!
Pier out from the main, let me catch myself with you, and
    stay – I will not chafe you,
I feel ashamed to go naked about the world.

I am curious to know where my feet stand – and what this is
      flooding me, childhood or manhood – and the hunger
      that crosses the bridge between.

8

The cloth laps a first sweet eating and drinking,
Laps life-swelling yolks – laps ear of rose-corn, milky and
      just ripen'd;
The white teeth stay, and the boss-tooth advances in darkness,
And liquor is spill'd on lips and blossoms by touching glasses,
      and the best liquor afterward.

9

I descent my western course, my sinews are flaccid,
Perfume and youth course through me, and I am their wake.

It is my face yellow and wrinkled, instead of the old woman's,
I sit low in a straw-bottom chair, and carefully darn my
      grandson's stockings.

It is I too, the sleepless widow, looking out of the winter
      midnight,
I see the sparkles of starshine on the icy and pallid earth.

A shroud I see, and I am the shroud – I wrap a body, and lie in
      the coffin,
It is dark here under ground – it is not evil or pain here – it is
      blank here, for reasons.

It seems to me that everything in the light and air ought
     to be happy,
Whoever is not in his coffin and the dark grave, let him know
     he has enough.

10

I see a beautiful gigantic swimmer, swimming naked through
     the eddies of the sea,
His brown hair lies close and even to his head—he strikes out
     with courageous arms—he urges himself with his legs,
I see his white body—I see his undaunted eyes,
I hate the swift-running eddies that would dash him head-fore-
     most on the rocks.

What are you doing, you ruffianly red-trickled waves?
Will you kill the courageous giant? Will you kill him in the
     prime of his middle age?

Steady and long he struggles,
He is baffled, bang'd, bruis'd—he holds out while his strength
     holds out,
The slapping eddies are spotted with his blood—they bear him
     away—they roll him, swing him, turn him,
His beautiful body is borne in the circling eddies, it is
     continually bruis'd on rocks,
Swiftly and out of sight is borne the brave corpse.

11

I turn, but do not extricate myself,
Confused, a past-reading, another, but with darkness yet.

The beach is cut by the razory ice-wind – the wreck-
        guns sound,
The tempest lulls – the moon comes floundering through
        the drifts.

I look where the ship helplessly heads end on – I hear the
        burst as she strikes – I hear the howls of dismay – they
        grow fainter and fainter.

I cannot aid with my wringing fingers,
I can but rush to the surf, and let it drench me and freeze
        upon me.

I search with the crowd – not one of the company is wash'd to
        us alive;
In the morning I help pick up the dead and lay them in rows
        in a barn.

12

Now of the older war-days, the defeat at Brooklyn,
Washington stands inside the lines – he stands on the
        intrench'd hills, amid a crowd of officers,
His face is cold and damp – he cannot repress the
        weeping drops,
He lifts the glass perpetually to his eyes – the color is blanch'd
        from his cheeks,
He sees the slaughter of the southern braves confided to him
        by their parents.

The same, at last and at last, when peace is declared,
He stands in the room of the old tavern – the well-belov'd
        soldiers all pass through,

The officers speechless and slow draw near in their turns,
The chief encircles their necks with his arm, and kisses them
    on the cheek,
He kisses lightly the wet cheeks one after another – he shakes
    hands, and bids good-by to the army.

13

Now I tell what my mother told me to-day as we sat at
    dinner together,
Of when she was a nearly grown girl, living home with her
    parents on the old homestead.

A red squaw came one breakfast time to the old homestead,
On her back she carried a bundle of rushes for rush-bottoming
    chairs,
Her hair, straight, shiny, coarse, black, profuse, half-envelop'd
    her face,
Her step was free and elastic, and her voice sounded
    exquisitely as she spoke.

My mother look'd in delight and amazement at the stranger,
She look'd at the freshness of her tall-borne face, and full and
    pliant limbs,
The more she look'd upon her, she loved her,
Never before had she seen such wonderful beauty and purity,
She made her sit on a bench by the jamb of the fireplace – she
    cook'd food for her,
She had no work to give her, but she gave her remembrance
    and fondness.

The red squaw staid all the forenoon, and toward the middle
    of the afternoon she went away,

O my mother was loth to have her go away!
All the week she thought of her – she watch'd for her many
         a month,
She remember'd her many a winter and many a summer,
But the red squaw never came, nor was heard of there again.

14

Now Lucifer was not dead – or if he was, I am his sorrowful
         terrible heir;
I have been wrong'd – I am oppress'd – I hate him that
         oppresses me,
I will either destroy him, or he shall release me.

Damn him! how he does defile me!
How he informs against my brother and sister, and takes pay
         for their blood!
How he laughs when I look down the bend, after the
         steamboat that carries away my woman!

Now the vast dusk bulk that is the whale's bulk, it seems mine;
Warily, sportsman! though I lie so sleepy and sluggish, the tap
         of my flukes is death.

15

A show of the summer softness! a contact of something
         unseen! an amour of the light and air!
I am jealous, and overwhelm'd with friendliness,
And will go gallivant with the light and air myself,
And have an unseen something to be in contact with
         them also.

O love and summer! you are in the dreams, and in me!
Autumn and winter are in the dreams – the farmer goes with
      his thrift,
The droves and crops increase, and the barns are well-fill'd.

16

Elements merge in the night – ships make tacks in the dreams,
The sailor sails – the exile returns home,
The fugitive returns unharm'd – the immigrant is back beyond
      month and years,
The poor Irishman lives in the simple house of his childhood,
      with the well-known neighbors and faces,
They warmly welcome him – he is barefoot again, he forgets he
      is well off;
The Dutchman voyages home, and the Scotchman and
      Welshman voyage home, and the native of the
      Mediterranean voyages home,
To every port of England, France, Spain, enter well-fill'd ships,
The Swiss foots it toward his hills – the Prussian goes his way,
      the Hungarian his way, and the Pole his way,
The Swede returns, and the Dane and Norwegian return.

17

The homeward bound, and the outward bound,
The beautiful lost swimmer, the ennuyé, the onanist, the
      female that loves unrequited, the money-maker,
The actor and actress, those through with their parts, and
      those waiting to commence,
The affectionate boy, the husband and wife, the voter, the
      nominee that is chosen, and the nominee that
      has fail'd,

The great already known, and the great any time after to-day,
The stammerer, the sick, the perfect-form'd, the homely,
The criminal that stood in the box, the judge that sat and
      sentenced him, the fluent lawyers, the jury,
      the audience,
The laugher and weeper, the dancer, the midnight widow, the
      red squaw,
The consumptive, the erysipelite, the idiot, he that is wrong'd,
The antipodes, and every one between this and them in
      the dark,
I swear they are averaged now—one is no better than the other,
The night and sleep have liken'd them and restored them.

I swear they are all beautiful;
Everyone that sleeps is beautiful—everything in the dim light
      is beautiful,
The wildest and bloodiest is over, and all is peace.

18

Peace is always beautiful,
The myth of heaven indicates peace and night.

The myth of heaven indicates the Soul;
The Soul is always beautiful—it appears more or it appears
      less—it comes, or it lags behind,
It comes from its embower'd garden, and looks pleasantly on
      itself, and encloses the world,
Perfect and clean the genitals previously jetting, and perfect
      and clean the womb cohering,
The head well-grown, proportion'd and plumb, and the bowels
      and joints proportion'd and plumb.

19

The Soul is always beautiful,
The universe is duly in order, everything is in its place,
What has arrived is in its place, and what waits is in its place;
The twisted skull waits, the watery of rotten blood waits,
The child of the glutton or venerealee waits long, and the
>child of the drunkard waits long, and the drunkard
>himself waits long,
The sleepers that lived and died wait – the far advanced are to
>go on in their turns, and the far behind are to come on
>in their turns,
The diverse shall be no less diverse, but they shall flow and
>unite – they unite now.

20

The sleepers are very beautiful as they lie unclothed,
They flow hand in hand over the whole earth, from east to
>west, as they lie unclothed,
The Asiatic and African are hand in hand – the European and
>American are hand in hand,
Learn'd and unlearn'd are hand in hand, and male and female
>are hand in hand,
The bare arm of the girl crosses the bare breast of her lover –
>they press close without lust – his lips press her neck,
The father holds his grown or ungrown son in his arms with
>measureless love, and the son holds the father in his
>arms with measureless love,
The white hair of the mother shines on the white wrist of
>the daughter,
The breath of the boy goes with the breath of the man, friend
>is inarm'd by friend,

The scholar kisses the teacher, and the teacher kisses the
      scholar – the wrong'd is made right,
The call of the slave is one with the master's call, and the
      master salutes the slave,
The felon steps forth from the prison – the insane becomes
      sane – the suffering of sick persons is reliev'd,
The sweatings and fevers stop – the throat that was unsound is
      sound – the lungs of the consumptive are resumed – the
      poor distress'd head is free,
The joints of the rheumatic move as smoothly as ever, and
      smoother than ever,
Stiflings and passages open – the paralyzed become supple,
The swell'd and convuls'd and congested awake to themselves
      in condition,
They pass the invigoration of the night, and the chemistry of
      the night, and awake.

21

I too pass from the night,
I stay a while away, O night, but I return to you again,
      and love you.

Why should I be afraid to trust myself to you?
I am not afraid – I have been well brought forward by you;
I love the rich running day, but I do not desert her in whom I
      lay so long,
I know not how I came of you, and I know not where I go with
      you – but I know I came well, and shall go well.

I will stop only a time with the night, and rise betimes;
I will duly pass the day, O my mother, and duly return to you.

CAROL OF WORDS

First published in 1856 under title of "Poem of The Sayers of the Words of The Earth"

1

EARTH, ROUND, ROLLING, compact – suns, moons, animals – all
    these are words to be said;
Watery, vegetable, sauroid advances – beings, premonitions,
    lispings of the future,
Behold! these are vast words to be said.

Were you thinking that those were the words – those upright
    lines? those curves, angles, dots?
No, those are not the words – the substantial words are in the
    ground and sea,
They are in the air – they are in you.

Were you thinking that those were the words – those delicious
    sounds out of your friends' mouths?
No, the real words are more delicious than they.

Human bodies are words, myriads of words;
In the best poems re-appears the body, man's or woman's, well-
    shaped, natural, gay,
Every part able, active, receptive, without shame or the need
    of shame.

2

Air, soil, water, fire – these are words;
I myself am a word with them – my qualities interpenetrate
        with theirs – my name is nothing to them;
Though it were told in the three thousand languages, what
        would air, soil, water, fire, know of my name?

A healthy presence, a friendly or commanding gesture, are
        words, sayings, meanings;
The charms that go with the mere looks of some men and
        women, are sayings and meanings also.

3

The workmanship of souls is by the inaudible words of
        the earth;
The great masters know the earth's words, and use them more
        than the audible words.

Amelioration is one of the earth's words;
The earth neither lags nor hastens;
It has all attributes, growths, effects, latent in itself from
        the jump;
It is not half beautiful only – defects and excrescences show
        just as much as perfections show.

The earth does not withhold, it is generous enough;
The truths of the earth continually wait, they are not so
        conceal'd either;
They are calm, subtle, untransmissible by print;
They are imbued through all things, conveying themselves
        willingly,

Conveying a sentiment and invitation of the earth – I utter
        and utter,
I speak not, yet if you hear me not, of what avail am I to you?
To bear – to better – lacking these, of what avail am I?

4

Accouche! Accouchez!
Will you rot your own fruit in yourself there?
Will you squat and stifle there?

The earth does not argue,
Is not pathetic, has no arrangements,
Does not scream, haste, persuade, threaten, promise,
Makes no discriminations, has no conceivable failures,
Closes nothing, refuses nothing, shuts none out,
Of all the powers, objects, states, it notifies, shuts none out.

5

The earth does not exhibit itself, nor refuse to exhibit itself –
        possesses still underneath;
Underneath the ostensible sounds, the august chorus of
        heroes, the wail of slaves,
Persuasions of lovers, curses, gasps of the dying, laughter of
        young people, accents of bargainers,
Underneath these, possessing the words that never fail.

To her children, the words of the eloquent dumb great mother
        never fail;
The true words do not fail, for motion does not fail, and
        reflection does not fail;
Also the day and night do not fail, and the voyage we pursue
        does not fail.

6

On the interminable sisters,
Of the ceaseless cotillions of sisters,
Of the centripetal and centrifugal sisters, the elder and
        younger sisters,
The beautiful sister we know dances on with the rest.

With her ample back towards every beholder,
With the fascinations of youth, and the equal fascinations
        of age,
Sits she whom I too love like the rest – sits undisturb'd,
Holding up in her hand what has the character of a mirror,
        while her eyes glance back from it,
Glance as she sits, inviting none, denying none,
Holding a mirror day and night tirelessly before her own face.

7

Seen at hand, or seen at a distance,
Duly the twenty-four appear in public every day,
Duly approach and pass with their companions, or a
        companion,
Looking from no countenances of their own, but from the
        countenances of those who are with them,
From the countenances of children or women, or the
        manly countenance,
From the open countenances of animals, or from
        inanimate things,
From the landscape or waters, or from the exquisite
        apparition of the sky,

From our countenances, mine and yours, faithfully
    returning them,
Every day in public appearing without fail, but never twice
    with the same companions.

8

Embracing man, embracing all, proceed the three hundred and
    sixty-five resistlessly round the sun;
Embracing all, soothing, supporting, follow close three
    hundred and sixty-five offsets of the first, sure and
    necessary as they.

9

Tumbling on steadily, nothing dreading,
Sunshine, storm, cold, heat, forever withstanding,
    passing, carrying,
The Soul's realization and determination still inheriting,
The fluid vacuum around and ahead still entering
    and dividing,
No balk retarding, no anchor anchoring, on no rock striking,
Swift, glad, content, unbereav'd, nothing losing,
Of all able and ready at any time to give strict account,
The divine ship sails the divine sea.

10

Whoever you are! motion and reflection are especially for you;
The divine ship sails the divine sea for you.

Whoever you are! you are he or she for whom the earth is
    solid and liquid,
You are he or she for whom the sun and moon hang in
    the sky,

For none more than you are the present and the past,
For none more than you is immortality.

11

Each man to himself, and each woman to herself, such
          is the word of the past and present, and the word of
          immortality;
No one can acquire for another – not one!
Not one can grow for another – not one!

The song is to the singer, and comes back most to him;
The teaching is to the teacher, and comes back most to him;
The murder is to the murderer, and comes back most to him;
The theft is to the thief, and comes back most to him;
The love is to the lover, and comes back most to him;
The gift is to the giver, and comes back most to him – it
          cannot fail;
The oration is to the orator, the acting is to the actor and
          actress, not to the audience;
And no man understands any greatness or goodness but his
          own, or the indication of his own.

12

I swear the earth shall surely be complete to him or her who
          shall be complete!
I swear the earth remains jagged and broken only to him or
          her who remains jagged and broken!
I swear there is no greatness or power that does not emulate
          those of the earth!
I swear there can be no theory of any account, unless it
          corroborate the theory of the earth!

No politics, art, religion, behavior, or what not, is of account,
        unless it compare with the amplitude of the earth,
Unless it face the exactness, vitality, impartiality, rectitude of
    the earth.

13

I swear I begin to see love with sweeter spasms than that
        which responds love!
It is that which contains itself—which never invites, and
    never refuses.

I swear I begin to see little or nothing in audible words!
I swear I think all merges toward the presentation of the
        unspoken meanings of the earth!
Toward him who sings the songs of the Body, and of the truths
        of the earth;
Toward him who makes the dictionaries of words that print
    cannot touch.

14

I swear I see what is better than to tell the best;
It is always to leave the best untold.

When I undertake to tell the best, I find I cannot,
My tongue is ineffectual on its pivots,
My breath will not be obedient to its organs,
I become a dumb man.

The best of the earth cannot be told anyhow—all or any
        is best;
It is not what you anticipated—it is cheaper, easier, nearer;

Things are not dismiss'd from the places they held before;
The earth is just as positive and direct as it was before;
Facts, religions, improvements, politics, trades, are as real
          as before;
But the Soul is also real,—it too is positive and direct;
No reasoning, no proof has establish'd it,
Undeniable growth has establish'd it.

15

This is a poem—a carol of words—these are hints of meanings,
These are to echo the tones of Souls,and the phrases of Souls;
If they did not echo the phrases of Souls, what were they then?
If they had not reference to you in especial, what were
          they then?

I swear I will never henceforth have to do with the faith that
          tells the best!
I will have to do only with that faith that leaves the
          best untold.

16

Say on, sayers!
Delve! mould! pile the words of the earth!
Work on—(it is materials you must bring, not breaths;)
Work on, age after age! nothing is to be lost;
It may have to wait long, but it will certainly come in use;
When the materials are all prepared, the architects
          shall appear.

I swear to you the architects shall appear without fail! I
        announce them and lead them;
I swear to you they will understand you, and justify you;
I swear to you the greatest among them shall be he who best
        knows you, and encloses all, and is faithful to all;
I swear to you, he and the rest shall not forget you – they shall
        perceive that you are not an iota less than they;
I swear to you, you shall be glorified in them.

THERE WAS A CHILD WENT FORTH

First published in 1855

THERE WAS A child went forth every day;
And the first object he look'd upon, that object he became;
And that object became part of him for the day, or a certain
        part of the day, or for many years, or stretching cycles
        of years.

The early lilacs became part of this child,
And grass, and white and red morning-glories, and white and
        red clover, and the song of the phœbe-bird,
And the Third-month lambs, and the sow's pink-faint litter,
        and the mare's foal, and the cow's calf,
And the noisy brood of the barn-yard, or by the mire of the
        pond-side,
And the fish suspending themselves so curiously below
        there – and the beautiful curious liquid,

And the water-plants with their graceful flat heads – all became
      part of him.

The field-sprouts of Fourth-month and Fifth-month became
      part of him;
Winter-grain sprouts, and those of the light-yellow corn, and
      the esculent roots of the garden,
And the apple-trees cover'd with blossoms, and the fruit
      afterward, and wood-berries, and the commonest
      weeds by the road;
And the old drunkard staggering home from the out-house of
      the tavern, whence he had lately risen,
And the school-mistress that pass'd on her way to the school,
And the friendly boys that pass'd – and the quarrelsome boys,
And the tidy and fresh-cheek'd girls – and the barefoot negro
      boy and girl,
And all the changes of city and country, wherever he went.

His own parents,
He that had father'd him, and she that had conceiv'd him in
      her womb, and birth'd him,
They gave this child more of themselves than that;
They gave him afterward every day – they became part of him.

The mother at home, quietly placing the dishes on the
      supper-table;
The mother with mild words – clean her cap and gown, a
      wholesome odor falling off her person and clothes as
      she walks by;
The father, strong, self-sufficient, manly, mean, anger'd, unjust;

The blow, the quick loud word, the tight bargain, the
          crafty lure,
The family usages, the language, the company, the furniture –
          the yearning and swelling heart,
Affection that will not be gainsay'd – the sense of what is real –
          the thought if, after all, it should prove unreal,
The doubts of day-time and the doubts of night-time – the
          curious whether and how,
Whether that which appears so is so, or is it all flashes
          and specks?
Men and women crowding fast in the streets – if they are not
          flashes and specks, what are they?
The streets themselves, and the facades of houses, and goods
          in the windows,
Vehicles, teams, the heavy-plank'd wharves – the huge crossing
          at the ferries,
The village on the highland, seen from afar at sunset – the
          river between,
Shadows, aureola and mist, the light falling on roofs and
          gables of white or brown, three miles off,
The schooner near by, sleepily dropping down the tide – the
          little boat slack-tow'd astern,
The hurrying tumbling waves, quick-broken crests, slapping,
The strata of color'd clouds, the long bar of maroon tint,
          away solitary by itself – the spread of purity it lies
          motionless in,
The horizon's edge, the flying sea-crow, the fragrance of salt
          marsh and shore mud;
These became part of that child who went forth every day, and
          who now goes, and will always go forth every day.

DRUM-TAPS

First published in "Drum-Taps," 1865

1

FIRST, O SONGS, for a prelude,
Lightly strike on the stretch'd tympanum, pride and joy in my
        city,
How she led the rest to arms—how she gave the cue,
How at once with lithe limbs, unwaiting a moment, she
        sprang;
(O superb! O Manhattan, my own, my peerless!
O strongest you in the hour of danger, in crisis! O truer
        than steel!)
How you sprang! how you threw off the costumes of peace
        with indifferent hand;
How your soft opera-music changed, and the drum and fife
        were heard in their stead;
How you led to the war, (that shall serve for our prelude, songs
        of soldiers,)
How Manhattan drum-taps led.

2

Forty years had I in my city seen soldiers parading;
Forty years as a pageant—till unawares, the Lady of this
        teeming and turbulent city,
Sleepless amid her ships, her houses, her incalculable wealth,
With her million children around her—suddenly,
At dead of night, at news from the south,
Incens'd, struck with clench'd hand the pavement.

A shock electric—the night sustain'd it;
Till with ominous hum, our hive at day-break pour'd out
        its myriads.

From the houses then, and the workshops, and through
      all the doorways,
Leapt they tumultuous – and lo! Manhattan arming.

3

To the drum-taps prompt,
The young men falling in and arming;
The mechanics arming, (the trowel, the jack-plane, the black-
      smith's hammer, tost aside with precipitation;)
The lawyer leaving his office, and arming – the judge leaving
      the court;
The driver deserting his wagon in the street, jumping down,
      throwing the reins abruptly down on the horses' backs;
The salesman leaving the store – the boss, book-keeper, porter,
      all leaving;
Squads gather everywhere by common consent, and arm;
The new recruits, even boys – the old men show them how
      to wear their accoutrements – they buckle the
      straps carefully;
Outdoors arming – indoors arming – the flash of the
      musket-barrels;
The white tents cluster in camps – the arm'd sentries around –
      the sunrise cannon, and again at sunset;
Arm'd regiments arrive every day, pass through the city, and
      embark from the wharves;
(How good they look, as they tramp down to the river, sweaty,
      with their guns on their shoulders!
How I love them! how I could hug them, with their brown
      faces, and their clothes and knapsacks cover'd
      with dust!)
The blood of the city up – arm'd! arm'd! the cry everywhere;

The flags flung out from the steeples of churches, and from all
      the public buildings and stores;
The tearful parting–the mother kisses her son–the son kisses
      his mother;
(Loth is the mother to part–yet not a word does she speak to
      detain him;)
The tumultuous escort–the ranks of policemen preceding,
      clearing the way;
The unpent enthusiasm–the wild cheers of the crowd for
      their favorites;
The artillery–the silent cannons, bright as gold, drawn along,
      rumble lightly over the stones;
(Silent cannons–soon to cease your silence!
Soon, unlimber'd, to begin the red business;)
All the mutter of preparation–all the determin'd arming;
The hospital service–the lint, bandages, and medicines;
The women volunteering for nurses–the work begun for, in
      earnest– no mere parade now;
War! an arm'd race is advancing!–the welcome for battle–no
      turning away;
War! be it weeks, months, or years–an arm'd race is advancing
      to welcome it.

4

Mannahatta a-march!–and it's O to sing it well!
It's O for a manly life in the camp!
And the sturdy artillery!
The guns, bright as gold–the work for giants–to serve well
      the guns:
Unlimber them! no more, as the past forty years, for salutes for
      courtesies merely;
Put in something else now besides powder and wadding.

5

And you, Lady of Ships! you Mannahatta!
Old matron of this proud, friendly, turbulent city!
Often in peace and wealth you were pensive, or covertly
       frown'd amid all your children;
But now you smile with joy, exulting old Mannahatta!

As I Sat Alone by Blue Ontario's Shore

First published in 1856 under title of "Poem of Many in One"

1

As I sat alone, by blue Ontario's shore,
As I mused of these mighty days, and of peace return'd, and
       the dead that return no more,
A Phantom, gigantic, superb, with stern visage, accosted me;
Chant me the poem, it said, *that comes from the soul of*
       America—chant me the carol of victory;
And strike up the marches of Libertad—marches more
       powerful yet;
And sing me before you go, the song of the throes of Democracy.

(Democracy—the destin'd conqueror—yet treacherous lip-
       smiles everywhere,
And Death and infidelity at every step.)

2

A Nation announcing itself,
I myself make the only growth by which I can be appreciated,
I reject none, accept all, then reproduce all in my own forms.

A breed whose proof is in time and deeds;
What we are, we are—nativity is answer enough to objections;
We wield ourselves as a weapon is wielded,
We are powerful and tremendous in ourselves,
We are executive in ourselves—We are sufficient in the variety
    of ourselves,
We are the most beautiful to ourselves, and in ourselves;
We stand self-pois'd in the middle, branching thence over
    the world;
From Missouri, Nebraska, or Kansas, laughing attacks to scorn.

Nothing is sinful to us outside of ourselves,
Whatever appears, whatever does not appear, we are beautiful
    or sinful in ourselves only.

(O mother! O sisters dear!
If we are lost, no victor else has destroy'd us;
It is by ourselves we go down to eternal night.)

3

Have you thought there could be but a single Supreme?
There can be any number of Supremes—One does not
    counter-vail another, any more than one eyesight
    countervails another, or one life countervails another.

All is eligible to all,
All is for individuals—All is for you,
No condition is prohibited—not God's, or any.

All comes by the body—only health puts you rapport with
    the universe.

Produce great persons, the rest follows.

4

America isolated I sing;
I say that works made here in the spirit of other lands, are so
    much poison in The States.

(How dare such insects as we see assume to write poems
    for America?
For our victorious armies, and the offspring following
    the armies?)

Piety and conformity to them that like!
Peace, obesity, allegiance, to them that like!
I am he who tauntingly compels men, women, nations,
Crying, Leap from your seats, and contend for your lives!

I am he who walks the States with a barb'd tongue, questioning
    every one I meet;
Who are you, that wanted only to be told what you knew before?
Who are you, that wanted only a book to join you in your
    nonsense?

(With pangs and cries, as thine own, O bearer of many children!
These clamors wild, to a race of pride I give.)

O lands! would you be freer than all that has ever been before?
If you would be freer than all that has been before, come listen
          to me.

Fear grace – Fear elegance, civilization, delicatesse,
Fear the mellow sweet, the sucking of honey-juice;
Beware the advancing mortal ripening of nature,
Beware what precedes the decay of the ruggedness of states
          and men.

5

Ages, precedents, have long been accumulating undirected
          materials,
America brings builders, and brings its own styles.

The immortal poets of Asia and Europe have done their work,
          and pass'd to other spheres,
A work remains, the work of surpassing all they have done.

America, curious toward foreign characters, stands by its own
          at all hazards,
Stands removed, spacious, composite, sound – initiates the true
          use of precedents,
Does not repel them, or the past, or what they have produced
          under their forms,
Takes the lesson with calmness, perceives the corpse slowly
          borne from the house,

Perceives that it waits a little while in the door – that it was
    fittest for its days,
That its life has descended to the stalwart and well-shaped
    heir who approaches,
And that he shall be fittest for his days.

Any period, one nation must lead,
One land must be the promise and reliance of the future.

These States are the amplest poem,
Here is not merely a nation, but a teeming nation of nations,
Here the doings of men correspond with the broadcast doings
    of the day and night,
Here is what moves in magnificent masses, careless of
    particulars,
Here are the roughs, beards, friendliness, combativeness, the
    Soul loves,
Here the flowing trains – here the crowds, equality, diversity,
    the Soul loves.

6

Land of lands, and bards to corroborate!
Of them, standing among them, one lifts to the light his west-
    bred face,
To him the hereditary countenance bequeath'd, both mother's
    and father's,
His first parts substances, earth, water, animals, trees,
Built of the common stock, having room for far and near,
Used to dispense with other lands, incarnating this land,
Attracting it Body and Soul to himself, hanging on its neck
    with incomparable love,
Plunging his seminal muscle into its merits and demerits,

Making its cities, beginnings, events, diversities, wars,
      vocal in him,
Making its rivers, lakes, bays, embouchure in him,
Mississippi with yearly freshets and changing chutes—
      Columbia, Niagara, Hudson, spending themselves
      lovingly in him,
If the Atlantic coast stretch, or the Pacific coast stretch, he
      stretching with them north or south,
Spanning between them, east and west, and touching whatever
      is between them,
Growths growing from him to offset the growth of pine, cedar,
      hemlock, live-oak, locust, chestnut, hickory, cotton-
      wood, orange, magnolia,
Tangles as tangled in him as any cane-brake or swamp,
He likening sides and peaks of mountains, forests coated with
      northern transparent ice,
Off him pasturage, sweet and natural as savanna, upland,
      prairie,
Through him flights, whirls, screams, answering those of the
      fish-hawk, mocking-bird, night-heron, and eagle;
His spirit surrounding his country's spirit, unclosed to good
      and evil,
Surrounding the essence of real things, old times and present
      times,
Surrounding just found shores, islands, tribes of red
      aborigines,
Weather-beaten vessels, landings, settlements, embryo stature
      and muscle,
The haughty defiance of the Year 1—war, peace, the formation
      of the Constitution,
The separate States, the simple, elastic scheme, the immigrants,
The Union, always swarming with blatherers, and always sure
      and impregnable,

The unsurvey'd interior, log houses, clearings, wild animals,
      hunters, trappers;
Surrounding the multiform agriculture, mines, temperature,
      the gestation of new States,
Congress convening every Twelfth-month, the members duly
      coming up from the uttermost parts;
Surrounding the noble character of mechanics and farmers,
      especially the young men,
Responding their manners, speech, dress, friendships – the gait
      they have of persons who never knew how it felt to
      stand in the presence of superiors,
The freshness and candor of their physiognomy, the
      copiousness and decision of their phrenology,
The picturesque looseness of their carriage, their fierceness
      when wrong'd,
The fluency of their speech, their delight in music, their
      curiosity, good temper, and open-handedness – the
      whole composite make,
The prevailing ardor and enterprise, the large amativeness,
The perfect equality of the female with the male, the fluid
      movement of the population,
The superior marine, free commerce, fisheries, whaling,
      gold-digging,
Wharf-hemm'd cities, railroad and steamboat lines, intersecting
      all points,
Factories, mercantile life, labor-saving machinery, the north-
      east, north-west, south-west,
Manhattan firemen, the Yankee swap, southern plantation life,
Slavery – the murderous, treacherous conspiracy to raise it
      upon the ruins of all the rest;
On and on to the grapple with it – Assassin! then your life or
      ours be the stake – and respite no more.

7

(Lo! high toward heaven, this day,
Libertad! from the conqueress' field return'd,
I mark the new aureola around your head;
No more of soft astral, but dazzling and fierce,
With war's flames, and the lambent lightnings playing,
And your port immovable where you stand;
With still the inextinguishable glance, and the clench'd and
      lifted fist,
And your foot on the neck of the menacing one, the scorner,
      utterly crush'd beneath you;
The menacing, arrogant one, that strode and advanced with
      his senseless scorn, bearing the murderous knife;
–Lo! the wide swelling one, the braggart, that would yesterday
      do so much!
To-day a carrion dead and damn'd, the despised of
      all the earth!
An offal rank, to the dunghill maggots spurn'd.)

8

Others take finish, but the Republic is ever constructive, and
      ever keeps vista;
Others adorn the past–but you, O days of the present,
      I adorn you!
O days of the future, I believe in you! I isolate myself for
      your sake;
O America, because you build for mankind, I build for you!
O well beloved stone-cutters! I lead them who plan with
      decision and science,
I lead the present with friendly hand toward the future.

Bravas to all impulses sending sane children to the next age!
But damn that which spends itself, with no thought of the
     stain, pains, dismay, feebleness it is bequeathing.

9

I listened to the Phantom by Ontario's shore,
I heard the voice arising, demanding bards;
By them, all native and grand—by them alone can The States
     be fused into the compact organism of a Nation.

To hold men together by paper and seal, or by compulsion, is
     no account;
That only holds men together which aggregates all in a living
     principle, as the hold of the limbs of the body, or the
     fibres of plants.

Of all races and eras, These States, with veins full of poetical
     stuff, most need poets, and are to have the greatest,
     and use them the greatest;
Their Presidents shall not be their common referee so much as
     their poets shall.

(Soul of love, and tongue of fire!
Eye to pierce the deepest deeps, and sweep the world!
—Ah, mother! prolific, and full in all besides—yet how long
     barren, barren?)

10

Of These States, the poet is the equable man,
Not in him, but off from him, things are grotesque, eccentric,
     fail of their full returns,
Nothing out of its place is good, nothing in its place is bad,

He bestows on every object or quality its fit proportion,
        neither more nor less,
He is the arbiter of the diverse, he is the key,
He is the equalizer of his age and land,
He supplies what wants supplying—he checks what
        wants checking,
In peace, out of him speaks the spirit of peace, large, rich,
        thrifty, building populous towns, encouraging
        agriculture, arts, commerce, lighting the study of man,
        the Soul, health, immortality, government;
In war, he is the best backer of the war—he fetches artillery as
        good as the engineer's—he can make every word he
        speaks draw blood;
The years straying toward infidelity, he withholds by his
        steady faith,
He is no argurer, he is judgment—(Nature accepts him
        absolutely;)
He judges not as the judge judges, but as the sun falling round
        a helpless thing;
As he sees the farthest, he has the most faith,
His thoughts are the hymns of the praise of things,
In the dispute of God and eternity he is silent,
He sees eternity less like a play with a prologue and
        denouement,
He sees eternity in men and women—he does not see men and
        women as dreams or dots.

For the great Idea, the idea of perfect and free individuals,
For that idea the bard walks in advance, leader of leaders,
The attitude of him cheers up slaves and horrifies
        foreign despots.

Without extinction is Liberty! without retrograde is Equality!
They live in the feelings of young men, and the best women;
Not for nothing have the indomitable heads of the earth been
    always ready to fall for Liberty.

11

For the great Idea!
That, O my brethren—that is the mission of Poets.

Songs of stern defiance, ever ready,
Songs of the rapid arming, and the march,
The flag of peace quick-folded, and instead, the flag we know,
Warlike flag of the great Idea.

(Angry cloth I saw there leaping!
I stand again in leaden rain, your flapping folds saluting;
I sing you over all, flying, beckoning through the fight—O the
    hard-contested fight!
O the cannons ope their rosy-flashing muzzles! the hurtled
    balls scream!
The battle-front forms amid the smoke—the volleys pour
    incessant from the line;
Hark! the ringing word, *Charge!*—now the tussle, and the
    furious maddening yells;
Now the corpses tumble curl'd upon the ground,
Cold, cold in death, for precious life of you,
Angry cloth I saw there leaping.)

12

Are you he who would assume a place to teach, or be a poet
    here in The States?
The place is august—the terms obdurate.

Who would assume to teach here, may well prepare himself,
       body and mind,
He may well survey, ponder, arm, fortify, harden, make
       lithe, himself,
He shall surely be question'd beforehand by me with many and
       stern questions.

Who are you, indeed, who would talk or sing to America?
Have you studied out the land, its idioms and men?
Have you learn'd the physiology, phrenology, politics,
       geography, pride, freedom, friendship, of the land? its
       sub-stratums and objects?
Have you consider'd the organic compact of the first day of the
       first year of Independence, sign'd by the
       Commissioners, ratified by The States, and read by
       Washington at the head of the army?
Have you possess'd yourself of the Federal Constitution?
Do you see who have left all feudal processes and poems
       behind them, and assumed the poems and processes
       of Democracy?
Are you faithful to things? do you teach as the land and sea,
       the bodies of men, womanhood, amativeness,
       angers, teach?
Have you sped through fleeting customs, popularities?
Can you hold your hand against all seductions, follies, whirls,
       fierce contentions? are you very strong? are you really
       of the whole people?
Are you not of some coterie? some school or mere religion?
Are you done with reviews and criticisms of life? animating
       now to life itself?
Have you vivified yourself from the maternity of These States?

Have you too the old, ever-fresh forbearance and impartiality?
Do you hold the like love for those hardening to maturity; for
the last-born? little and big? and for the errant?

What is this you bring my America?
Is it uniform with my country?
Is it not something that has been better told or done before?
Have you not imported this, or the spirit of it, in some ship?
Is it not a mere tale? a rhyme? a prettiness? is the good old
cause in it?
Has it not dangled long at the heels of the poets, politicians,
literats, of enemies' lands?
Does it not assume that what is notoriously gone is still here?
Does it answer universal needs? will it improve manners?
Does it sound, with trumpet-voice, the proud victory of the
Union, in that secession war?
Can your performance face the open fields and the seaside?
Will it absorb into me as I absorb food, air – to appear again in
my strength, gait, face?
Have real employments contributed to it? original makers – not
mere amanuenses?
Does it meet modern discoveries, calibers, facts face to face?
What does it mean to me? to American persons, progresses,
cities? Chicago, Kanada, Arkansas? the planter, Yankee,
Georgian, native, immigrant, sailors, squatters, old
States, new States?
Does it encompass all The States, and the unexceptional rights
of all the men and women of the earth? (the genital
impulse of These States;)

Does it see behind the apparent custodians, the real
          custodians, standing, menacing, silent—the mechanics,
          Manhattanese, western men, southerners, significant
          alike in their apathy, and in the promptness of
          their love?
Does it see what finally befalls, and has always finally befallen,
          each temporizer, patcher, outsider, partialist, alarmist,
          infidel, who has ever ask['d anything of America?
What mocking and scornful negligence?
The track strew'd with the dust of skeletons;
By the roadside others disdainfully toss'd.

13

Rhymes and rhymers pass away—poems distill'd from foreign
          poems pass away,
The swarms of reflectors and the polite pass, and leave ashes;
Admirers, importers, obedient persons, make but the soul of
          literature;
America justifies itself, give it time—no disguise can deceive it,
          or conceal from it—it is impassive enough,
Only toward the likes of itself will it advance to meet them,
If its poets appear, it will in due time advance to meet them—
          there is no fear of mistake,
(The proof of a poet shall be sternly deferr'd, till his country
          absorbs him as affectionately s he has absorb'd it.)

He masters whose spirit masters—he tastes sweetest who
          results sweetest in the long run;
The blood of the brawn beloved of time is unconstraint;

In the need of poems, philosophy, politics, manners,
       engineering, an appropriate native and grand-opera,
       shipcraft, any craft, he or she is greatest who
       contributes the greatest original practical example.

Already a nonchalant breed, silently emerging, appears on
       the streets,
People's lips salute only doers, lovers, satisfiers, positive knowers;
There will shortly be no more priests—I say their work
       is done,
Death is without emergencies here, but life is perpetual
       emergencies here,
Are your body, days, manners, superb? after death you
       shall be superb;
Justice, health, self-esteem, clear the way with
       irresistible power;
How dare you place anything before a man?

14

Fall behind me, States!
A man before all—myself, typical before all.

Give me the pay I have served for!
Give me to sing the song of the great Idea! take all the rest;
I have loved the earth, sun, animals—I have despised riches,
I have given alms to every one that ask'd, stood up for the
       stupid and crazy, devoted my income and labor
       to others,
I have hated tyrants, argued not concerning God, had patience
       and indulgence toward the people, taken off my hat to
       nothing known or unknown,

I have gone freely with powerful uneducated persons, and with
      the young, and with the mothers of families,
I have read these leaves to myself in the open air—I have tried
      them by trees, stars, rivers,
I have dismiss'd whatever insulted my own Soul or defiled
      my Body,
I have claim'd nothing to myself which I have not carefully
      claim'd for others on the same terms,
I have sped to the camps, and comrades found and accepted
      from every State;
(In war of you, as well as peace, my suit is good, America—
      sadly I boast;
Upon this breast has many a dying soldier lean'd, to breathe
      his last;
This arm, this hand, this voice, have nourish'd, rais'd, restored,
To life recalling many a prostrate form:)
—I am willing to wait to be understood by the growth of the
      taste of myself,
I reject none, I permit all.

(Say, O mother! have I not to your thought been faithful?
Have I not, through life, kept you and yours before me?)

15

I swear I begin to see the meaning of these things!
It is not the earth, it is not America, who is so great,
It is I who am great, or to be great—it is you up there,
      or any one;
It is to walk rapidly through civilizations, governments,
      theories,
Through poems, pageants, shows, to form great individuals.

Underneath all, individuals!
I swear nothing is good to me now that ignores individuals,
The American compact is altogether with individuals,
The only government is that which makes minute of
      individuals,
The whole theory of the universe is directed to one single
      individual—namely, to You.

(Mother! with subtle sense severe—with the naked sword in
      your hand,
I saw you at last refuse to treat but directly with individuals.)

16

Underneath all, nativity,
I swear I will stand by me own nativity—pious or impious,
      so be it;
I swear I am charm'd with nothing except nativity,
Men, women, cities, nations, are only beautiful from nativity.

Underneath all is the need of the expression of love for men
      and women,
I swear I have seen enough of mean and impotent modes of
      expressing love for men and women,
After this day I take my own modes of expressing love for men
      and women.

I swear I will have each quality of my race in myself,
(Talk as you like, he only suits These States whose manners
      favor the audacity and sublime turbulence of
      The States.)

Underneath the lessons of things, spirits, Nature, governments,
      ownerships, I swear I perceive other lessons,
Underneath all, to me is myself – to you, yourself – (the same
      monotonous old song.)

17

O I see now, flashing, that this America is only you and me,
Its power, weapons, testimony, are you and me,
Its crimes, lies, thefts, defections, slavery, are you and me,
Its Congress is you and me – the officers, capitols, armies,
      ships, are you and me,
Its endless gestations of new States are you and me,
The war – that war so bloody and grim – the war I will hence-
      forth forget – was you and me,
Natural and artificial are you and me,
Freedom, language, poems, employments, are you and me,
Past, present, future, are you and me.

18

I swear I dare not shirk any part of myself,
Not any part of America, good or bad,
Not the promulgation of Liberty – not to cheer up slaves and
      horrify foreign despots,
Not to build for that which builds for mankind,
Not to balance ranks, complexions, creeds, and the sexes,
Not to justify science, nor the march of equality,
Nor to feed the arrogant blood of the brawn beloved of time.

I swear I am for those that have never been master'd!
For men and women whose tempers have never been master'd,
For those whom laws, theories, conventions, can never master.

I swear I am for those who walk abreast with the whole earth!
Who inaugurate one, to inaugurate all.

I swear I will not be outfaced by irrational things!
I will penetrate what it is in them that is sarcastic upon me!
I will make cities and civilizations defer to me!
This is what I have learnt from America—it is the amount—and
       it I teach again.

(Democracy! while weapons were everywhere aim'd at
       your breast,
I saw you serenely give birth to immortal children—saw in
       dreams your dilating form;
Saw you with spreading mantle covering the world.)

19

I will confront these shows of the day and night!
I will know if I am to be less than they!
I will see if I am not as majestic as they!
I will see if I am not as subtle and real as they!
I will see if I am to be less generous than they!
I will see if I have no meaning, while the houses and ships
       have meaning!
I will see if the fishes and birds are to be enough for
       themselves, and I am not to be enough for myself.

20

I match my spirit against yours, you orbs, growths,
       mountains, brutes,
Copious as you are, I absorb you all in myself, and become
       the master myself.

America isolated, yet embodying all, what is it finally
          except myself?
These States—what are they except myself?

I know now why the earth is gross, tantalizing, wicked—it is
          for my sake,
I take you to be mine, you beautiful, terrible, rude forms.

(Mother! bend down, bend close to me your face!
I know not what these plots and wars, and deferments are for;
I know not fruition's success—but I know that through war and
          peace your work goes on, and must yet go on.)

21

. . . . Thus, by blue Ontario's shore,
While the winds fann'd me, and the waves came trooping
          toward me,
I thrill'd with the Power's pulsations—and the charm of my
          theme was upon me,

Till the tissues that held me, parted their ties upon me.
And I saw the free Souls of poets;
The loftiest bards of past ages strode before me,
Strange, large men, long unwaked, undisclosed, were disclosed
          to me.

22

O my rapt verse, my call—mock me not!
Not for the bards of the past—not to invoke them have I
          launch'd you forth,
Not to call even those lofty bards here by Ontario's shores,
Have I sung so capricious and loud, my savage song.

Bards for my own land, only, I invoke;
(For the war, the war is over – the field is clear'd,)
Till they strike up marches henceforth triumphant
        and onward,
To cheer, O mother, your boundless, expectant soul.

Bards grand as these days so grand!
Bards of the great Idea! Bards of the peaceful inventions! (for
        the war, the war is over!)
Yet Bards of the latent armies – a million soldiers waiting,
        ever-ready,
Bards towering like hills – (no more these dots, these pigmies,
        these little piping straws, these gnats, that fill the hour,
        to pass for poets;)
Bards with songs as from burning coals, or the lightning's
        fork'd stripes!
Ample Ohio's bards – bards for California! inland bards – bards
        of the war;)
(As a wheel turns on its axle, so I find my chants turning
        finally on the war;)
Bards of pride! Bards tallying the ocean's roar, and the
        swooping eagle's scream!
You, by my charm, I invoke!

MANNAHATTA

First published in 1860

I WAS ASKING for something specific and perfect for my city,
Whereupon, lo! upsprang the aboriginal name!

Now I see what there is in a name, a word, liquid, sane,
          unruly, musical, self-sufficient;
I see that the word of my city is that word up there,
Because I see that word nested in nests of water-bays, superb,
          with tall and wonderful spires,
Rich, hemm'd thick all around with sailships and
          steamships—an island sixteen miles long,
          solid-founded,
Numberless crowded streets—high growths of iron, slender,
          strong, light, splendidly uprising toward clear skies;
Tide swift and ample, well-loved by me, toward sundown,
The flowing sea-currents, the little islands, larger adjoining
          islands, the heights, the villas,
The countless masts, the white shore-steamers, the lighters, the
          ferry-boats, the black sea-steamers well-model'd;
The down-town streets, the jobbers' houses of business—the
          houses of business of the ship-merchants, and money-
          brokers—the river-streets;
Immigrants arriving, fifteen or twenty thousand in a week;
The carts hauling goods—the manly race of drivers of
          horses—the brown-faced sailors;
The summer air, the bright sun shining, and the sailing
          clouds aloft;
The winter snows, the sleigh-bells—the broken ice in the river
          passing along, up or down, with the flood tide or
          ebb-tide;
The mechanics of the city, the masters, well-form'd, beautiful-
          faced, looking you straight in the eyes;
Trottoirs throng'd—vehicles—Broadway—the women—the shops
          and shows,

The parades, processions, bugles playing, flags flying,
        drums beating;
A million people—manners free and superb—open voices—
        hospitality—the most courageous and friendly
        young men;
The free city! no slaves! no owners of slaves!
The beautiful city, the city of hurried and sparkling waters! the
        city of spires and masts!
The city nested in bays! my city!
The city of such women, I am mad to be with them! I will
        return after death to be with them!
The city of such young men, I swear I cannot live happy,
        without I often go talk, walk, eat, drink, sleep,
        with them!

Passage to India

First published in 1870

1

Singing my days,
Singing the great achievements of the present,
Singing the strong, light works of engineers,
Our modern wonders, (the antique ponderous Seven outvied,)
In the Old World, the east, the Suez canal,
The New by its mighty railroad spann'd,
The seas inlaid with eloquent, gentle wires,
I sound, to commence, the cry, with thee, O soul,
The Past! the Past! the Past!

The Past! the dark, unfathom'd retrospect!
The teeming gulf! the sleepers and the shadows!
The past! the infinite greatness of the past!
For what is the present, after all, but a growth out of the past?
(As a projectile, form'd, impell'd passing a certain line, still
        keeps on,
So the present, utterly form'd, impell'd by the past.)

2

Passage, O soul, to India!
Eclaircise the myths Asiatic – the primitive fables.

Not you alone, proud truths of the world!
Nor you alone, ye facts of modern science!
But myths and fables of eld – Asia's, Africa's fables!
The far-darting beams of the spirit! – the unloos'd dreams!
The deep diving bibles and legends;
The daring plots of the poets – the elder religions;
– O you temples fairer than lilies, pour'd over by the
        rising sun!
O you fables, spurning the known, eluding the hold of the
        known, mounting to heaven!
You lofty and dazzling towers, pinnacled, red as roses,
        burnish'd with gold!
Towers of fables immortal, fashion'd from mortal dreams!
You too I welcome, and fully, the same as the rest;
You too with joy I sing.

3

Passage to India!
Lo, soul! seest thou not God's purpose from the first?
The earth to be spann'd, connected by net-work,

The people to become brothers and sisters,
The races, neighbors, to marry and be given in marriage,
The oceans to be cross'd, the distant brought near,
The lands to be welded together.

(A worship new, I sing;
You captains, voyagers, explorers, yours!
You engineers! you architects, machinists, yours!
You, not for trade or transportation only,
But in God's name, and for thy sake, O soul.)

4

Passage to India!
Lo, soul, for thee, of tableaus twain,
I see, in one, the Suez canal initiated, open'd,
I see the procession of steamships, the Empress Eugenie's
        leading the van;
I mark, from on deck, the strange landscape, the pure sky, the
        level sand in the distance;
I pass swiftly the picturesque groups, the workmen gather'd,
The gigantic dredging machines.

In one, again, different, (yet thine, all thine, O soul, the same,)
I see over my own continent the Pacific Railroad, surmounting
        every barrier;
I see continual trains of cars winding along the Platte, carrying
        freight and passengers;
I hear the locomotives rushing and roaring, and the shrill
        steam-whistle,
I hear the echoes reverberate through the grandest scenery in
        the world;

I cross the Laramie plains—I note the rocks in grotesque
          shapes—the buttes;
I see the plentiful larkspur and wild onions—the barren, color-
          less, sage-deserts;
I see in glimpses afar, or towering immediately above me, the
          great mountains—I see the Wind River and the
          Wahsatch mountains;
I see the Monument mountain and the Eagle's Nest—I pass the
          Promontory—I ascend the Nevadas;
I scan the noble Elk mountain, and wind around its base;
I see the Humboldt range—I thread the valley and cross
          the river,
I see the clear waters of Lake Tahoe—I see forests of
          majestic pines,
Or, crossing the great desert, the alkaline plains, I behold
          enchanting mirages of waters and meadows;
Marking through these, and after all, in duplicate slender lines,
Bridging the three or four thousand miles of land travel,
Tying the Eastern to the Western sea,
The road between Europe and Asia.

(Ah Genoese, thy dream! thy dream!
Centuries after thou art laid in thy grave,
The shore thou foundest verifies thy dream!)

5

Passage to India!
Struggles of many a captain—tales of many a sailor dead!
Over my mood, stealing and spreading they come,
Like clouds and cloudlets in the unreach'd sky.

Along all history, down the slopes,
As a rivulet running, sinking now, and now again to the
          surface rising,
A ceaseless thought, a varied train—Lo, soul! to thee, thy sight,
          they rise,
The plans, the voyages again, the expeditions:
Again Vasco de Gama sails forth;
Again the knowledge gain'd, the mariner's compass,
Lands found, and nations born—thou born, America,
          (a hemisphere unborn,)
For purpose vast, man's long probation fill'd,
Thou, rondure of the world, at last accomplish'd.

6

O, vast Rondure, swimming in space!
Cover'd all over with visible power and beauty!
Alternate light and day, and the teeming, spiritual darkness;
Unspeakable, high processions of sun and moon, and
          countless stars, above;
Below, the manifold grass and waters, animals, mountains, trees;
With inscrutable purpose—some hidden, prophetic intention;
Now, first, it seems, my thought begins to span thee.

Down from the gardens of Asia, descending, radiating,
Adam and Eve appear, then their myriad progeny after them,
Wandering, yearning, curious—with restless explorations,
With questionings, baffled, formless, feverish—with never-
          happy hearts,
With that sad, incessant refrain, *Wherefore, unsatisfied Soul?*
          and *Whither, O mocking Life?*

Ah, who shall soothe these feverish children?
Who justify these restless explorations?
Who speak the secret of impassive Earth?
Who bind it to us? What is this separate Nature, so unnatural?
What is this Earth, to our affections? (unloving earth, without
          a throb to answer ours;
Cold earth, the place of graves.)

Yet, soul, be sure the first intent remains – and shall be
          carried out;
(Perhaps even now the time has arrived.)

After the seas are all cross'd, (as they seem already cross'd,)
After the great captains and engineers have accomplish'd
          their work,
After the noble inventors – after the scientists, the chemist, the
          geologist, ethnologist,
Finally shall come the Poet, worthy that name;
The true Son of God shall come, singing his songs.

Then, not your deeds only, O voyagers, O scientists and
          inventors, shall be justified,
All these hearts, as of fretted children, shall be sooth'd,
All affection shall be fully responded to – the secret shall
          be told;
All these separations and gaps shall be taken up, and hook'd
          and link'd together;
The whole Earth – this cold, impassive, voiceless Earth, shall
          be completely justified;
Trinitas divine shall be gloriously accomplish'd and compacted
          by the true Son of God, the poet,

(He shall indeed pass the straits and conquer the mountains,
He shall double the Cape of Good Hope to some purpose;)
Nature and Man shall be disjoin'd and diffused no more,
The true Son of God shall absolutely fuse them.

7

Year at whose open'd, wide-flung door I sing!
Year of the purpose accomplish'd!
Year of the marriage of continents, climates and oceans!
(No mere Doge of Venice now, wedding the Adriatic;)
I see, O year, in you, the vast terraqueous globe, given, and
          giving all,
Europe to Asia, Africa join'd, and they to the New World;
The lands, geographies, dancing before you, holding a
          festival garland,
As brides and bridegrooms hand in hand.

8

Passage to India!
Cooling airs from Caucasus far, soothing cradle of man,
The river Euphrates flowing, the past lit up again.

Lo, soul, the retrospect, brought forward;
The old, most populous, wealthiest of Earth's lands,
The streams of the Indus and the Ganges, and their
          many affluents;
(I, my shores of America walking to-day, behold, resuming all,)
The tale of Alexander, on his warlike marches, suddenly dying,
On one side China, and on the other side Persia and Arabia,
To the south the great seas, and the Bay of Bengal;
The flowing literatures, tremendous epics, religions, castes,

Old occult Brahma, interminably far back—the tender and
    junior Buddha,
Central and southern empires, and all their belongings,
    possessors,
The wars of Tamerlane, the reign of Aurungzebe,
The traders, rulers, explorers, Moslems, Venetians, Byzantium,
    the Arabs, Portuguese,
The first travelers, famous yet, Marco Polo, Batouta the Moor,
Doubts to be solv'd, the map incognita, blanks to be fill'd,
The foot of man unstay'd, the hands never at rest,
Thyself, O soul, that will not brook a challenge.

9

The medieval navigators rise before me,
The world of 1492, with its awaken'd enterprise;
Something swelling in humanity now like the sap of the earth
    in spring,
The sunset splendor of chivalry declining.

And who art thou, sad shade?
Gigantic, visionary, thyself a visionary,
With majestic limbs, and pious, beaming eyes,
Spreading around, with every look of thine, a golden world,
Enhuing it with gorgeous hues.

As the chief histrion,
Down to the footlights walks, in some great scena,
Dominating the rest, I see the Admiral himself,
(History's type of courage, action, faith;)
Behold him sail from Palos, leading his little fleet;
His voyage behold—his return—his great fame,

His misfortunes, calumniators—behold him a prisoner, chain'd,
Behold his dejection, poverty, death.

(Curious, in time, I stand, noting the efforts of heroes;
Is the deferment long? bitter the slander, poverty, death?
Lies the seed unreck'd for centuries in the ground? Lo! to
          God's due occasion,
Uprising in the night, it sprouts, blooms,
And fills the earth with use and beauty.)

10

Passage indeed, O soul, to primal thought!
Not lands and seas alone—thy own clear freshness,
The young maturity of brood and bloom;
To realms of budding bibles.

O soul, repressless, I with thee, and thou with me,
Thy circumnavigation of the world begin;
Of man, the voyage of his mind's return,
To reason's early paradise,
Back, back to wisdom's birth, to innocent intuitions,
Again with fair Creation.

11

O we can wait no longer!
We too take ship, O soul!
Joyous, we too launch out on trackless seas!
Fearless, for unknown shores, on waves of extasy to sail,
Amid the wafting winds, (thou pressing me to thee, I thee to
          me, O soul,)
Caroling free—singing our song of God,
Chanting our chant of pleasant exploration.

With laugh, and many a kiss,
(Let others deprecate – Let others weep for sin, remorse,
          humiliation;)
O soul, thou pleasest me – I thee.

Ah, more than any priest, O soul, we too believe in God;
But with the mystery of God we dare not dally.

O soul, thou pleasest me – I thee;
Sailing these seas, or on the hills, or waking in the night,
Thoughts, silent thoughts, of Time, and Space, and Death, like
          waters flowing,
Bear me, indeed, as through the regions infinite,
Whose air I breathe, whose ripples hear – lave me all over;
Bathe me, O God, in thee – mounting to thee,
I and my soul to range in range of thee.

O Thou transcendant!
Nameless – the fibre and the breath!
Light of the light – shedding forth universes – thou centre
          of them!
Thou mightier centre of the true, the good, the loving!
Thou moral, spiritual fountain! affection's source!
          thou reservoir!
(O pensive soul of me! O thirst unsatisfied! waitest not there?
Waitest not haply for us, somewhere there, the Comrade
          perfect?)
Thou pulse! thou motive of the stars, suns, systems,
That, circling, move in order, safe, harmonious,
Athwart the shapeless vastnesses of space!

How should I think—how breathe a single breath—how
          speak—if, out of myself,
I could not launch, to those, superior universes?

Swiftly I shrivel at the thought of God,
At Nature and its wonders, Time and Space and Death,
But that I, turning, call to thee, O soul, thou actual Me,
And lo! thou gently masterest the orbs,
Thou matest Time, smilest content at Death,
And fillest, swellest full, the vastnesses of Space.

Greater than stars or suns,
Bounding, O soul, thou journeyest forth;
—What love, than thine and ours could wider amplify?
What aspirations, wishes, outvie thine and ours, O soul?
What dreams of the ideal? what plans of purity,
          perfection, strength?
What cheerful willingness, for others' sake, to give up all?
For others' sake to suffer all?

Reckoning ahead, O soul, when thou, the time achiev'd,
(The seas all cross'd, weather'd the capes, the voyage done,)
Surrounded, copest, frontest God, yieldest, the aim attain'd,
As, fill'd with friendship, love complete, the Elder
          Brother found,
The Younger melts in fondness in his arms.

12

Passage to more than India!
Are thy wings plumed indeed for such far flights?
O Soul, voyagest thou indeed on voyages like these?

Disportest thou on waters such as these?
Soundest below the Sanscrit and the Vedas?
They have thy bent unleash'd.

Passage to you, your shores, ye aged fierce enigmas!
Passage to you, to mastership of you, ye strangling problems!
You, strew'd with the wrecks of skeletons, that, living, never
      reach'd you.

13

Passage to more than India!
O secret of the earth and sky!
Of you, O waters of the sea! O winding creeks and rivers!
Of you, O woods and fields! Of you, strong mountains
      of my land!
Of you, O prairies! Of you, gray rocks!
O morning red! O clouds! O rain and snows!
O day and night, passage to you!

O sun and moon, and all you stars! Sirius and Jupiter!
Passage to you!

Passage—immediate passage! the blood burns in my veins!
Away, O soul! hoist instantly the anchor!
Cut the hawsers—haul out—shake out every sail!
Have we not stood here like trees in the ground long enough?
Have we not grovell'd here long enough, eating and drinking
      like mere brutes?
Have we not darken'd and dazed ourselves with books
      long enough?

Sail forth! steer for the deep waters only!
Reckless, O soul, exploring, I with thee, and thou with me;
For we are bound where mariner has not yet dared to go,
And we will risk the ship, ourselves and all.

O my brave soul!
O farther, farther sail!
O daring joy, but safe! Are they not all the seas of God?
O farther, farther, farther sail!

PROUD MUSIC OF THE STORM

First published in 1870

1

PROUD MUSIC OF the storm!
Blast that careers so free, whistling across the prairies!
Strong hum of forest tree-tops! Wind of the mountains!
Personified dim shapes! you hidden orchestras!
You serenades of phantoms, with instruments alert,
Blending, with Nature's rhythmus, all the tongues of nations;
You chords left us by vast composers! you choruses!
You formless, free, religious dances! you from the Orient!
You undertone of rivers, roar of pouring cataracts;
You sounds from distant guns, with galloping cavalry!
        Echoes of camps, with all the different bugle-calls!
Trooping tumultuous, filling the midnight late, bending
        me powerless,
Entering my lonesome slumber-chamber—Why have you
        seiz'd me?

2

Come forward, O my Soul, and let the rest retire;
Listen – lose not – it is toward thee they tend;
Parting the midnight, entering my slumber-chamber,
For thee they sing and dance, O Soul.

A festival song!
The duet of the bridegroom and the bride – a marriage-march,
With lips of love, and hearts of lovers, fill'd to the brim
        with love;
The red-flush'd cheeks, and perfumes – the cortege swarming,
        full of friendly faces, young and old,
To flutes' clear notes, and sounding harps' cantabile.

3

Now loud approaching drums!
Victoria! see'st thou in powder-smoke the banners torn but
        flying? the rout of the baffled?
Hearest those shouts of a conquering army?

(Ah, Soul, the sobs of women – the wounded groaning in agony,
The hiss and crackle of flames – the blacken'd ruins – the
        embers of cities,
The dirge and desolation of mankind.)

4

Now airs antique and medieval fill me!
I see and hear old harpers with their harps, at Welsh festivals:
I hear the minnesingers, singing their lays of love,
I hear the minstrels, gleemen, troubadours, of the feudal ages.

5

Now the great organ sounds,
Tremulous–while underneath, (as the hid footholds of
        the earth,
On which arising, rest, and leaping forth, depend,
All shapes of beauty, grace and strength–all hues we know,
Green blades of grass, and warbling birds–children that
        gambol and play–the clouds of heaven above,)
The strong base stands, and its pulsations intermits not,
Bathing, supporting, merging all the rest–maternity of all
        the rest;
And with it every instrument in multitudes,
The players playing–all the world's musicians,
The solemn hymns and masses, rousing adoration,
All passionate heart-chants, sorrowful appeals,
The measureless sweet vocalists of ages,
And for their solvent setting, Earth's own diapason,
Of winds and woods and mighty ocean waves;
A new composite orchestra–binder of years and climes–
        ten-fold renewer,
As of the far-back days the poets tell–the Paradiso,
The straying thence, the separation long, but now the
        wandering done,
The journey done, the Journeyman come home,
And Man and Art, with Nature fused again.

6

Tutti! for Earth and Heaven!
The Almighty Leader now for me, for once has signal'd with
        his wand.

The manly strophe of the husbands of the world,
And all the wives responding.

The tongues of violins!
(I think, O tongues, ye tell this heart, that cannot tell itself;
This brooding, yearning heart, that cannot tell itself.)

7

Ah, from a little child,
Thou knowest, Soul, how to me all sounds became music;
My mother's voice, in lullaby or hymn;
The voice – O tender voices – memory's loving voices!
Last miracle of all – O dearest mother's, sister's, voices;)
The rain, the growing corn, the breeze among the
      long-leav'd corn,
The measur'd sea-surf, beating on the sand,
The twittering bird, the hawk's sharp scream,
The wild-fowl's notes at night, as flying low, migrating north
      or south,
The psalm in the country church, or mid the clustering trees,
      the open air camp-meeting,
The fiddler in the tavern – the glee, the long-strung sailor-song,
The lowing cattle, bleating sheep – the crowing cock at dawn.

8

All songs of current lands come sounding 'round me,
The German airs of friendship, wine and love,
Irish ballads, merry jigs and dances – English warbles,
Chansons of France, Scotch tunes – and o'er the rest,
Italia's peerless compositions.

Across the stage, with pallor on her face, yet lurid passion,
Stalks Norma, brandishing the dagger in her hand.

I see poor crazed Lucia's eyes' unnatural gleam;
Her hair down her back falls loose and dishevell'd.

I see where Ernani, walking the bridal garden,
Amid the scent of night-roses, radiant, holding his bride
          by the hand,
Hears the infernal call, the death-pledge of the horn.

To crossing swords, and grey hairs bared to heaven,
The clear, electric base and baritone of the world,
The trombone duo—Libertad forever!

From Spanish chestnut trees' dense shade,
By old and heavy convent walls, a wailing song,
Song of lost love—the torch of youth and life quench'd
          in despair,
Song of the dying swan—Fernando's heart is breaking.

Awaking from her woes at last, retriev'd Amina sings;
Copious as stars, and glad as morning light, the torrents
          of her joy.

(The teeming lady comes!
The lustrious orb—Venus contralto—the blooming mother,
Sister of loftiest gods—Alboni's self I hear.)

9

I hear those odes, symphonies, operas;
I hear in the *William Tell,* the music of an arous'd and
        angry people;
I hear Meyerbeer's *Huguenots,* the *Prophet,* or *Robert;*
Gounod's *Faust,* or Mozart's *Don Juan.*

10

I hear the dance-music of all nations,
The waltz, (some delicious measure, lapsing, bathing me
        in bliss;)
The bolero, to tinkling guitars and clattering castanets.

I see religious dances old and new,
I hear the sound of the Hebrew lyre,
I see the Crusaders marching, bearing the cross on high, to the
        martial clang of cymbals;
I hear dervishes monotonously chanting, interspers'd with
        frantic shouts, as they spin around, turning always
        towards Mecca;
I see the rapt religious dances of the Persians and the Arabs;
Again, at Eleusis, home of Ceres, I see the modern
        Greeks dancing,
I hear them clapping their hands, as they bend their bodies,
I hear the metrical shuffling of their feet.

I see again the wild old Corybantian dance, the performers
        wounding each other;
I see the Roman youth, to the shrill sound of flageolets,
        throwing and catching their weapons,
As they fall on their knees, and rise again.

I hear from the Mussulman mosque the muezzin calling;
I see the worshippers within, (nor form, nor sermon,
        argument, nor word,
But silent, strange, devout—rais'd, glowing heads—extatic faces.)

11

I hear the Egyptian harp of many strings,
The primitive chants of the Nile boatmen;
The sacred imperial hymns of China,
To the delicate sounds of the king, (the stricken wood
        and stone;)
Or to Hindu flutes, and the fretting twang of the vina,
A band of bayaderes.

12

Now Asia, Africa leave me—Europe, seizing, inflates me;
To organs huge, and bands, I hear as from vast concourses
        of voices,
Luther's strong hymn, *Eine feste Burg ist unser Gott;*
Rossini's *Stabat Mater dolorosa;*
Or, floating in some high cathedral dim, with gorgeous
        color'd windows,
The passionate *Agnus Dei,* or *Gloria in Excelsis.*

13

Composers! mighty maestros!
And you, sweet singers of old lands—Soprani! Tenori! Bassi!
To you a new bard, carolling free in the west,
Obeisant, sends his love.

(Such led to thee, O Soul!
All senses, shows and objects, lead to thee,
But now, it seems to me, sound leads o'er all the rest.)

14

I hear the annual singing of the children in St. Paul's
        Cathedral;
Or, under the high roof of some colossal hall, thy symphonies,
        oratorios of Beethoven, Handel, or Haydn;
The *Creation*, in billows of godhood laves me.

Give me to hold all sounds, (I, madly struggling, cry,)
Fill me with all the voices of the universe,
Endow me with their throbbings—Nature's also,
The tempests, waters, winds—operas and chants—marches
        and dances,
Utter—pour in—for I would take them all.

15

Then I woke softly,
And pausing, questioning awhile the music of my dream,
And questioning all those reminiscences—the tempest in
        its fury,
And all the songs of sopranos and tenors,
And those rapt oriental dances, of religious fervor,
And the sweet varied instruments, and the diapason of organs,
And all the artless plaints of love, and grief and death,
I said to my silent, curious Soul, out of the bed of the
        slumber-chamber,
Come, for I have found the clue I sought so long,
Let us go forth refresh'd amid the day,

Cheerfully tallying life, walking the world, the real,
Nourish'd henceforth by our celestial dream.

And I said, moreover,
Haply, what thou hast heard, O Soul, was not the sound
       of winds,
Nor dream of raging storm, nor sea-hawk's flapping wings, nor
       harsh scream,
Nor vocalism of sun-bright Italy,
Nor German organ majestic — nor vast concourse of voices —
       nor layers of harmonies;
Nor strophes of husbands and wives — nor sound of
       marching soldiers,
Nor flutes, nor harps, nor the bugle-calls of camps;
But, to a new rhythmus fitted for thee,
Poems, bridging the way from Life to Death, vaguely wafted in
       night air, uncaught, unwritten,
Which, let us go forth in the bold day, and write.

WHEN LILACS LAST IN THE DOOR-YARD BLOOM'D

First published in "When Lilacs Last in the Door-yard Bloom'd," 1865–6

1

WHEN LILACS LAST in the door-yard bloom'd,
And the great star early droop'd in the western sky in
       the night,
I mourn'd — and yet shall mourn with ever-returning spring.

O ever-returning spring! trinity sure to me you bring;
Lilac blooming perennial, and drooping star in the west,
And thought of him I love.

2

O powerful, western, fallen star!
O shades of night! O moody, tearful night!
O great star disappear'd! O the black murk that hides the star!
O cruel hands that hold me powerless! O helpless soul of me!
O harsh surrounding cloud, that will not free my soul!

3

In the door-yard fronting an old farm-house, near the white-
      wash'd palings,
Stands the lilac bush, tall-growing, with heart-shaped leaves of
      rich green,
With many a pointed blossom, rising, delicate, with the
      perfume strong I love,
With every leaf a miracle . . . . . . and from this bush in the
      door-yard,
With delicate-color'd blossoms, and heart-shaped leaves of
      rich green,
A sprig, with its flower, I break.

4

In the swamp, in secluded recesses,
A shy and hidden bird is warbling a song.

Solitary, the thrush,
The hermit, withdrawn to himself, avoiding the settlements,
Sings by himself a song.

Song of the bleeding throat!
Death's outlet song of life—(for well, dear brother, I know,
If thou wast not gifted to sing, thou would'st surely die.)

5

Over the breast of the spring, the land, amid cities,
Amid lanes, and through old woods, (where lately the violets
        peep'd from the ground, spotting the gray debris;)
Amid the grass in the fields each side of the lanes—passing the
        endless grass;
Passing the yellow-spear'd wheat, every grain from its shroud
        in the dark-brown fields uprising;
Passing the apple-tree blows of white and pink in the orchards;
Carrying a corpse to where it shall rest in the grave,
Night and day journeys a coffin.

6

Coffin that passes through lanes and streets,
Through day and night, with the great cloud darkening
        the land,
With the pomp of the inloop'd flags, with the cities draped
        in black,
With the show of the States themselves, as of crape-veil'd
        women, standing,
With processions long and winding, and the flambeaus
        of the night,
With the countless torches lit—with the silent sea of faces,
        and the unbared heads,
With the waiting depot, the arriving coffin, and the
        sombre faces,

With dirges through the night, with the thousand voices rising
     strong and solemn;
With all the mournful voices of the dirges, pour'd around
     the coffin,
The dim-lit churches and the shuddering organs—Where amid
     these you journey,
With the tolling, tolling bells' perpetual clang;
Here! coffin that slowly passes,
I give you my sprig of lilac.

7

(Nor for you, for one, alone;
Blossoms and branches green to coffins all I bring:
For fresh as the morning—thus would I carol a song for you,
O sane and sacred death.

All over bouquets of roses,
O death! I cover you over with roses and early lilies;
But mostly and now the lilac that blooms the first,
Copious, I break, I break the sprigs from the bushes;
With loaded arms I come, pouring for you,
For you, and the coffins all of you, O death.)

8

O western orb, sailing the heaven!
Now I know what you must have meant, as a month since
     we walk'd,
As we walk'd up and down in the dark blue so mystic,
As we walk'd in silence the transparent shadowy night,
As I saw you had something to tell, as you bent to me night
     after night,

As you droop'd from the sky low down, as if to my side, (while
    the other stars all look'd on;)
As we wander'd together the solemn night, (for something, I
    know not what, kept me from sleep;)
As the night advanced, and I saw on the rim of the west, ere
    you went, how full you were of woe;
As I stood on the rising ground in the breeze, in the cold
    transparent night,
As I watch'd where you pass'd and was lost in the netherward
    black of the night,
As my soul, in its trouble, dissatisfied, sank, as where you,
    sad orb,
Concluded, dropt in the night, and was gone.

9

Sing on, there in the swamp!
O singer bashful and tender! I hear your notes—I hear
    your call;
I hear—I come presently—I understand you;
But a moment I linger—for the lustrous star has detain'd me;
The star, my departing comrade, holds and detains me.

10

O how shall I warble myself for the dead one there I loved?
And how shall I deck my song for the large sweet soul that
    has gone?
And what shall my perfume be, for the grave of him I love?

Sea-winds, blown from east and west,
Blown from the eastern sea, and blown from the western sea,
    till there on the prairies meeting:

These, and with these, and the breath of my chant,
I perfume the grave of him I love.

11

O what shall I hang on the chamber walls?
And what shall the pictures be that I hang on the walls,
To adorn the burial-house of him I love?

Pictures of growing spring, and farms, and homes,
With the Fourth-month eve at sundown, and the gray smoke
          lucid and bright,
With floods of the yellow gold of the gorgeous, indolent,
          sinking sun, burning, expanding the air;
With the fresh sweet herbage under foot, and the pale green
          leaves of the trees prolific;
In the distance the flowing glaze, the breast of the river, with a
          wind-dapple here and there;
With ranging hills on the banks, with many a line against the
          sky, and shadows;
And the city at hand, with dwellings so dense, and stacks
          of chimneys,
And all the scenes of life, and the workshops, and the
          workmen homeward returning.

12

Lo! body and soul! this land!
Mighty Manhattan, with spires, and the sparkling and hurrying
          tides, and the ships;
The varied and ample land – the South and the North in the
          light – Ohio's shores, and flashing Missouri,
And ever the far-spreading prairies, cover'd with grass
          and corn.

Lo! the most excellent sun, so calm and haughty;
The violet and purple morn, with just-felt breezes;
The gentle, soft-born, measureless light;
The miracle, spreading, bathing all—the fulfill'd noon;
The coming eve, delicious—the welcome night, and the stars,
Over my cities shining all, enveloping man and land.

13

Sing on! sing on, you gray-brown bird!
Sing from the swamps, the recesses—pour your chant from
          the bushes;
Limitless out of the dusk, out of the cedars and pines.

Sing on, dearest brother—warble your reedy song;
Loud human song, with voice of uttermost woe.

O liquid, and free, and tender!
O wild and loose to my soul! O wondrous singer!
You only I hear . . . . . . yet the star holds me, (but will
          soon depart;)
Yet the lilac, with mastering odor, holds me.

14

Now while I sat in the day, and look'd forth,
In the close of the day, with its light, and the fields of spring,
          and the farmer preparing his crops,
In the large unconscious scenery of my land, with its lakes
          and forests,
In the heavenly aerial beauty, (after the perturb'd winds, and
          the storms;)
Under the arching heavens of the afternoon swift passing, and
          the voices of children and women,

The many-moving sea-tides,—and I saw the ships how
      they sail'd,
And the summer approaching with richness, and the fields all
      busy with labor,
And the infinite separate houses, how they all went on, each
      with its meals and minutia of daily usages;
And the streets, how their throbbings throbb'd, and the cities
      pent—lo! then and there,
Falling upon them all, and among them all, enveloping me
      with the rest,
Appear'd the cloud, appear'd the long black trail;
And I knew Death, its thought, and the sacred knowledge
      of death.

15

Then with the knowledge of death as walking one side of me,
And the thought of death close-walking the other side of me,
And I in the middle, as with companions, and as holding the
      hands of companions,
I fled forth to the hiding receiving night, that talks not,
Down to the shores of the water, the path by the swamp in
      the dimness,
To the solemn shadowy cedars, and ghostly pines so still.

And the singer so shy to the rest receiv'd me;
The gray-brown bird I know, receiv'd us comrades three;
And he sang what seem'd the carol of death, and a verse for
      him I love.

From deep secluded recesses,
From the fragrant cedars, and the ghostly pines so still,
Came the carol of the bird.

And the charm of the carol rapt me,
As I held, as if by their hands, my comrades in the night;
And the voice of my spirit tallied the song of the bird.

16

DEATH CAROL

Come, lovely and soothing Death,
Undulate round the world, serenely arriving, arriving,
In the day, in the night, to all, to each,
Sooner or later, delicate Death.

Prais'd be the fathomless universe,
For life and joy, and for objects and knowledge curious;
And for love, sweet love—But praise! praise! praise!
For the sure-enwinding arms of cool-enfolding Death.

Dark Mother, always gliding near, with soft feet,
Have none chanted for thee a chant of fullest welcome?
Then I chant it for thee—I glorify thee above all;
I bring thee a song that when thou must indeed come, come
         unfalteringly.

Approach, strong Deliveress!
When it is so—when thou hast taken them, I joyously sing the
         dead,

Lost in the loving, floating ocean of thee,
Laved in the flood of thy bliss, O Death.

From me to thee glad serenades,
Dances for thee I propose, saluting thee—adornments and
*   feastings for thee;*
And the sights of the open landscape, and the high-spread sky, are
*   fitting,*
And life and the fields, and the huge and thoughtful night.

The night, in silence, under many a star;
The ocean shore, and the husky whispering wave, whose voice I
*   know;*
And the soul turning to thee, O vast and well-veil'd Death,
And the body gratefully nestling close to thee.

Over the tree-tops I float thee a song!
Over the rising and sinking waves—over the myriad fields, and the
*   prairies wide;*
Over the dense-pack'd cities all, and the teeming wharves and
*   ways,*
I float this carol with joy, with joy to thee, O Death!

17

To the tally of my soul,
Loud and strong kept up the gray-brown bird,
With pure, deliberate notes, spreading, filling the night.

Loud in the pines and cedars dim,
Clear in the freshness moist, and the swamp-perfume;
And I with my comrades there in the night.

While my sight that was bound in my eyes unclosed,
As to long panoramas of visions.

18

I saw askant the armies;
And I saw, as in noiseless dreams, hundreds of battle-flags;
Borne through the smoke of the battles, and pierc'd with
       missiles, I saw them,
And carried hither and yon through the smoke, and torn
       and bloody;
And at last but a few shreds left on the staffs, (and all in
       silence,)
And the staffs all splinter'd and broken.

I saw battle-corpses, myriads of them,
And the white skeletons of young men—I saw them;
I saw the debris and debris of all the dead soldiers of the war;
But I saw they were not as was thought;
They themselves were fully at rest—they suffer'd not;
The living remain'd and suffer'd—the mother suffer'd,
And the wife and the child, and the musing comrade suffer'd,
And the armies that remain'd suffer'd.

19

Passing the visions, passing the night;
Passing, unloosing the hold of my comrades' hands;
Passing the song of the hermit bird, and the tallying song of
       my soul,
(Victorious song, death's outlet song, yet varying,
       ever-altering song,
As low and wailing, yet clear the notes, rising and falling,
       flooding the night,

Sadly sinking and fainting, as warning and warning, and yet
  again bursting with joy,
Covering the earth, and filling the spread of the heaven,
As that powerful psalm in the night I heard from recesses,)
Passing, I leave thee, lilac with heart-shaped leaves;
I leave thee there in the door-yard, blooming, returning
  with spring.

I cease from my song for thee;
From my gaze on thee in the west, fronting the west,
  communing with thee,
O comrade lustrous, with silver face in the night.

20

Yet each I keep, and all, retrievements out of the night;
The song, the wondrous chant of the gray-brown bird,
And the tallying chant, the echo arous'd in my soul,
With the lustrous and drooping star, with the countenance full
  of woe,
With the lilac tall, and its blossoms of mastering odor;
With the holders holding my hand, nearing the call of
  the bird,
Comrades mine, and I in the midst, and their memory ever I
  keep—for the dead I loved so well;
For the sweetest, wisest soul of all my days and lands . . . and
  this for his dear sake;
Lilac and star and bird, twined with the chant of my soul,
There in the fragrant pines, and the cedars dusk and dim.

O Captain! My Captain!

First published in "When Lilacs Last in the Door-yard Bloom'd," 1865−6

1

O CAPTAIN! MY Captain! our fearful trip is done;
The ship has weather'd every rack, the prize we sought is won;
The port is near, the bells I hear, the people all exulting,
While follow eyes the steady keel, the vessel grim and daring:
    But O heart! heart! heart!
        O the bleeding drops of red,
            Where on the deck my Captain lies,
                Fallen cold and dead.

2

O Captain! my Captain! rise up and hear the bells;
Rise up−for you the flag is flung−for you the bugle trills;
For you bouquets and ribbon'd wreaths−for you the shores
        a-crowding;
For you they call, the swaying mass, their eager faces turning;
    Here Captain! dear father!
        This arm beneath your head;
            It is some dream that on the deck,
                You've fallen cold and dead.

3

My Captain does not answer, his lips are pale and still;
My father does not feel my arm, he has no pulse nor will;
The ship is anchor'd safe and sound, its voyage closed
        and done;

From fearful trip, the victor ship, comes in with object won:
    Exult, O shores, and ring, O bells!
        But I, with mournful tread,
           Walk the deck my Captain lies,
              Fallen cold and dead.

A NOISELESS, PATIENT SPIDER

First published in 1870

A NOISELESS, PATIENT spider,
I mark'd, where, on a little promontory, it stood, isolated;
Mark'd how, to explore the vacant, vast surrounding,
It launch'd forth filament, filament, filament, out of itself;
Ever unreeling them—ever tirelessly speeding them.

And you, O my Soul, where you stand,
Surrounded, surrounded, in measureless oceans of space,
Ceaselessly musing, venturing, throwing,—seeking the spheres,
        to connect them;
Till the bridge you will need, be form'd—till the ductile
        anchor hold;
Till the gossamer thread you fling, catch somewhere,
        O my Soul.

OUT OF THE CRADLE ENDLESSLY ROCKING

First published in 1860 and 1867 under title of "A Word Out of the Sea"

1

OUT OF THE cradle endlessly rocking,
Out of the mocking bird's throat, the musical shuttle,
Out of the Ninth-month midnight,
Over the sterile sands, and the fields beyond, where the child,
       leaving his bed, wander'd alone, bare-headed, barefoot,
       Down from the shower'd halo,
Up from the mystic play of shadows, twining and twisting as if
       they were alive,
Out from the patches of briers and blackberries,
From the memories of the bird that chanted to me,
From your memories, sad brother—from the fitful risings and
       fallings I heard,
From under that yellow half-moon, late-risen, and swollen as if
       with tears,
From those beginning notes of sickness and love, there in the
       transparent mist,
From the thousand responses of my heart, never to cease,
From the myriad thence-arous'd words,
From the word stronger and more delicious than any,
From such, as now they start, the scene revisiting,
As a flock, twittering, rising, or overhead passing,
Borne hither—ere all eludes me, hurriedly,
A man—yet by these tears a little boy again,
Throwing myself on the sand, confronting the waves,
I, chanter of pains and joys, uniter of here and hereafter,
Taking all hints to use them—but swiftly leaping beyond them,
A reminiscence sing.

2

Once, Paumanok,
When the snows had melted—when the lilac-scent was in the
      air, and the Fifth-month grass was growing,
Up this sea-shore, in some briers,
Two guests from Alabama—two together,
And their nest, and four light-green eggs, spotted with brown,
And every day the he-bird, to and from, near at hand,
And every day the she-bird, crouch'd on her nest, silent, with
      bright eyes,
And every day I, a curious boy, never too close, never
      disturbing them,
Cautiously peering, absorbing, translating.

3

Shine! shine! shine!
Pour down your warmth, great Sun!
While we bask—we two together.

Two together!
Winds blow South, or winds blow North,
Day come white, or night come black,
Home, or rivers and mountains from home,
Singing all time, minding no time,
While we two keep together.

4

Till of a sudden,
May-be kill'd, unknown to her mate,
One forenoon the she-bird crouch'd not on the nest,
Nor return'd that afternoon, nor the next,
Nor ever appear'd again.

And thenceforward, all summer, in the sound of the sea,
And at night, under the full of the moon, in calmer weather,
Over the hoarse surging of the sea,
Or flitting from brier to brier by day,
I saw, I heard at intervals, the remaining one, the he-bird,
The solitary guest from Alabama.

5

Blow! blow! blow!
Blow up, sea-winds, along Paumanok's shore!
I wait and I wait, till you blow my mate to me.

6

Yes, when the stars glisten'd,
All night long, on the prong of a moss-scallop'd stake,
Down, almost amid the slapping waves,
Sat the lone singer, wonderful, causing tears.

He call'd on his mate;
He pour'd forth the meanings which I, of all men, know.

Yes, my brother, I know;
The rest might not—but I have treasur'd every note;
For once, and more than once, dimly, down to the
          beach gliding,
Silent, avoiding the moonbeams, blending myself with
          the shadows,
Recalling now the obscure shapes, the echoes, the sounds and
          sights after their sorts,
The white arms out in the breakers tirelessly tossing,

I, with bare feet, a child, the wind wafting my hair,
Listen'd long and long.

Listen'd, to keep, to sing—not translating the notes,
Following you, my brother.

7

Soothe! soothe! soothe!
Close on its wave soothes the wave behind,
And again another behind, embracing and lapping, every
          one close,
But my love soothes not me, not me.

Low hangs the moon—it rose late;
O it is lagging—O I think it is heavy with love, with love.

O madly the sea pushes, pushes upon the land,
With love—with love.

O night! do I not see my love fluttering out there among the
          breakers?
What is that little black thing I see there in the white?

Loud! loud! loud!
Loud I call to you, my love!
High and clear I shoot my voice over the waves;
Surely you must know who is here, is here;
You must know who I am, my love.

Low-hanging moon!
What is that dusky spot in your brown yellow?
O it is the shape, the shape of my mate!
O moon, do not keep her from me any longer.

Land! land! O land!
Whichever way I turn, O I think you could give me my mate back
*   again, if you only would;*
For I am almost sure I see her dimly whichever way I look.

O rising stars!
Perhaps the one I want so much will rise, will rise with some
*   of you.*

O throat! O trembling throat!
Sound clearer through the atmosphere!
Pierce the woods, the earth;
Somewhere listening to catch you, must be the one I want.

Shake out, carols!
Solitary here—the night's carols!
Carols of lonesome love! Death's carols!
Carols under that lagging, yellow, waning moon!
O, under that moon, where she droops almost down into the sea!
O reckless, despairing carols.

But soft! sink low;
Soft! let me just murmur;
And do you wait a moment, you husky-noised sea;
For somewhere I believe I heard my mate responding to me,
So faint—I must be still, be still to listen;
But not altogether still, for then she might not come immediately
*   to me.*

Hither my love!
Here I am! Here!
With this just-sustain'd note I announce myself to you;
This gentle call is for you, my love, for you.

Do not be decoy'd elsewhere!
That is the whistle of the wind – it is not my voice;
That is the fluttering, the fluttering of the spray;
Those are the shadows of leaves.

O darkness! O in vain!
O I am very sick and sorrowful.

O brown halo in the sky, near the moon, drooping upon the sea!
O troubled reflection in the sea!
O throat! O throbbing heart!
O all – and I singing uselessly, uselessly all the night.

Yet I murmur, murmur on!
O murmurs – you yourselves make me continue to sing, I know
         not why.

O past! O life! O songs of joy!
In the air – in the woods – over fields;
Loved! loved! loved! loved! loved!
But my love no more, no more with me!
We two together no more.

8

The aria sinking;
All else continuing – the stars shining,

The winds blowing–the notes of the bird continuous echoing,
With angry moans the fierce old mother incessantly moaning,
On the sands of Paumanok's shore, gray and rustling;
The yellow half-moon enlarged, sagging down, drooping, the
            face of the sea almost touching;
The boy extatic–with his bare feet the waves, with his hair the
            atmosphere dallying,
The love in the heart long pent, now loose, now at last
            tumultuously bursting,
The aria's meaning, the ears, the Soul, swiftly depositing,
The strange tears down the cheeks coursing,
The colloquy there–the trio–each uttering,
The undertone–the savage old mother, incessantly crying,
To the boy's Soul's questions sullenly timing–some drown'd
            secret hissing,
To the outsetting bard of love.

9

Demon or bird! (said the boy's soul,)
Is it indeed toward your mate you sing? or is it mostly to me?
For I, that was a child, my tongue's use sleeping,
Now I have heard you,
Now in a moment I know what I am for–I awake,
And already a thousand singers–a thousand songs, clearer,
            louder and more sorrowful than yours,
A thousand warbling echoes have started to life within me,
Never to die.

O you singer, solitary, singing by yourself–projecting me;
O solitary me, listening–nevermore shall I cease
            perpetuating you;

Never more shall I escape, never more the reverberations,
Never more the cries of unsatisfied love be absent from me,
Never again leave me to be the peaceful child I was before
        what there, in the night,
By the sea, under the yellow and sagging moon,
The messenger there arous'd – the fire, the sweet hell within,
The unknown want, the destiny of me.

O give me the clew! (it lurks in the night here somewhere;)
O if I am to have so much, let me have more!
O a word! O what is my destination? (I fear it is
        henceforth chaos;)
O how joys, dreads, convolutions, human shapes, and all
        shapes, spring as from graves around me!
O phantoms! you cover all the land and all the sea!
O I cannot see in the dimness whether you smile or frown
        upon me;
O vapor, a look, a word! O well-beloved!
O you dear women's and men's phantoms!
A word then, (for I will conquer it,)
The word final, superior to all,
Subtle, sent up – what is it? – I listen;
Are you whispering it, and have been all the time, you
        sea-waves?
Is that it from your liquid rims and wet sands?

10

Whereto answering, the sea,
Delaying not, hurrying not,
Whisper'd me through the night, and very plainly before
        daybreak,
Lisp'd to me the low and delicious word DEATH;

And again Death–ever Death, Death, Death,
Hissing melodious, neither like the bird, nor like my arous'd
        child's heart,
But edging near, as privately for me, rustling at my feet,
Creeping thence steadily up to my ears, and laving me softly
        all over,
Death, Death, Death, Death, Death.

Which I do not forget,
But fuse the song of my dusky demon and brother,
That he sang to me in the moonlight on Paumanok's
        gray beach,
With the thousand responsive songs, at random,
My own songs, awaked from that hour;
And with them the key, the word up from the waves,
The word of the sweetest song, and all songs,
That strong and delicious word which, creeping to my feet,
The sea whisper'd me.

A CAROL OF HARVEST, FOR 1867

First published in 1870

1

A SONG OF the good green grass!
A song no more of the city streets;
As song of farms–a song of the soil of fields.

A song with the smell of sun-dried hay, where the nimble
　　　pitchers handle the pitch-fork;
A song tasting of new wheat, and of fresh-husk'd maize.

2

For the lands, and for these passionate days, and for myself,
Now I awhile return to thee, O soil of Autumn fields,
Reclining on thy breast, giving myself to thee,
Answering the pulses of thy sane and equable heart,
Tuning a verse for thee.

O Earth, that hast no voice, confide to me a voice!
O harvest of my lands! O boundless summer growths!
O lavish, brown, parturient earth! O infinite, teeming womb!
A verse to seek, to see, to narrate thee.

3

Ever upon this stage,
Is acted God's calm, annual drama,
Gorgeous processions, songs of birds,
Sunrise, that fullest feeds and freshens most the soul,
The heaving sea, the waves upon the shore, the musical,
　　　strong waves,
The woods, the stalwart trees, the slender, tapering trees,
The flowers, the grass, the lilliput, countless armies of
　　　the grass,
The heat, the showers, the measureless pasturages,
The scenery of the snows, the winds' free orchestra,
The stretching, light-hung roof of clouds – the clear cerulean,
　　　and the bulging, silvery fringes,
The high dilating stars, the placid, beckoning stars,

The moving flocks and herds, the plains and emerald
       meadows,
The shows of all the varied lands, and all the growths
       and products.

4

Fecund America! To-day,
Thou are all over set in births and joys!
Thou groan'st with riches! thy wealth clothes thee as with a
       swathing garment!
Thou laughest loud with ache of great possessions!
A myriad-twining life, like interlacing vines, binds all thy
       vast demesne!
As some huge ship, freighted to water's edge, thou ridest
       into port!
As rain falls from the heaven, and vapors rose from earth, so
       have the precious values fallen upon thee, and risen
       out of thee!
Thou envy of the glove! thou miracle!
Thou, bathed, choked, swimming in plenty!
Thou lucky Mistress of the tranquil barns!
Thou Prairie Dame that sittest in the middle, and lookest out
       upon thy world, and lookest East, and lookest West!
Dispensatress, that by a word givest a thousand miles – that
       giv'st a million farms, and missest nothing!
Thou All-Acceptress – thou Hospitable – (thou only art
       hospitable, as God is hospitable.)

5

When late I sang, sad was my voice;
Sad were the shows around me, with deafening noises of
       hatred, and smoke of conflict;

In the midst of the armies, the Heroes, I stood,
Or pass'd with slow step through the wounded and dying.

But now I sing not War,
Nor the measur'd march of soldiers, nor the tents of camps,
Nor the regiments hastily coming up, deploying in line
          of battle.

No more the dead and wounded;
No more the sad, unnatural shows of War.

Ask'd room those flush'd immortal ranks? the first forth-
          stepping armies?
Ask room, alas, the ghastly ranks—the armies dread
          that follow'd.

6

(Pass—pass, ye proud brigades!
So handsome, dress'd in blue—with your tramping,
          sinewy legs;
With your shoulders young and strong—with your knapsacks
          and your muskets;
—How elate I stood and watch'd you, where, starting off,
          you march'd!

Pass;—then rattle, drums, again!
Scream, you steamers on the river, out of whistles loud and
          shrill, your salutes!
For an army heaves in sight—O another gathering army!
Swarming, trailing on the rear—O you dread, accruing army!
O you regiments so piteous, with your mortal diarrhœa! with
          your fever!

O my land's maimed darlings! with the plenteous bloody
        bandage and the crutch!
Lo! your pallid army follow'd!)

7

But on these days of brightness,
On the far-stretching beauteous landscape, the roads and
        lanes, the high-piled farm-wagons, and the fruits
        and barns,
Shall the dead intrude?

Ah, the dead to me mar not—they fit well in Nature;
They fit very well in the landscape, under the trees and grass,
And along the edge of the sky, in the horizon's far margin.

Nor do I forget you, departed;
Nor in winter or summer, my lost ones;
But most, in the open air, as now, when my soul is rapt and at
        peace—like pleasing phantoms,
Your dear memories, rising, glide silently by me.

8

I saw the day, the return of the Heroes;
(Yet the Heroes never surpass'd, shall never return;
Them, that day, I saw not.)

I saw the interminable Corps—I saw the processions of armies,
I saw them approaching, defiling by, with divisions,
Streaming northward, their work done, camping awhile in
        clusters of mighty camps.

No holiday soldiers!—youthful, yet veterans;
Work, swart, handsome, strong, of the stock of homestead
          and workshop,
Harden'd of many a long campaign and sweaty march,
Inured on many a hard-fought, bloody field.

9

A pause—the armies wait;
A million flush'd, embattled conquerors wait;
The world, too, waits—then, soft as breaking night, as
          sure as dawn,
They melt—they disappear.

Exult, indeed, O lands! victorious lands!
Not there your victory, on those red, shuddering fields;
But here and hence your victory.

Melt, melt away ye armies! disperse, ye blue-clad soldiers!
Resolve ye back again—give up, for good, your deadly arms;
Other the arms, the fields henceforth for you, or South or
          North, or East or West,
With saner wars—sweet wars—life-giving wars.

10

Loud, O my throat, and clear, O soul!
The season of thanks, and the voice of full-yielding;
The chant of joy and power for boundless fertility.

All till'd and untill'd fields expand before me;
I see the true arenas of my race—or first, or last,
Man's innocent and strong arenas.

I see the Heroes at other toils;
I see, well-wielded in their hands, the better weapons.

11

I see where America, Mother of All,
Well-pleased, with full-spanning eye, gazes forth, dwells long,
And counts the varied gathering of the products.

Busy the far, the sunlit panorama;
Prairie, orchard, and yellow grain of the North,
Cotton and rice of the South, and Louisianian cane;
Open, unseeded fallows, rich fields of clover and timothy,
Kine and horses feeding, and droves of sheep and swine,
And many a stately river flowing, and many a jocund brook,
And healthy uplands with their herby-perfumed breezes,
And the good green grass – that delicate miracle, the ever-
          recurring grass.

12

Toil on, Heroes! harvest the products!
Not alone on those warlike fields, the Mother of All,
With dilated form and lambent eyes, watch'd you.

Toil on, Heroes! toil well! Handle the weapons well!
The Mother of All – yet here, as ever, she watches you.

Well-pleased, America, thou beholdest,
Over the fields of the West, those crawling monsters,
The human-divine inventions, the labor-saving implements:
Beholdest, moving in every direction, imbued as with life, the
          revolving hay-rakes,

The steam-power reaping-machines, and the horse-power
      machines,
The engines, thrashers of grain, and cleaners of grain, well
      separating the straw—the nimble work of the patent
      pitch-fork;
Beholdest the newer saw-mill, the southern cotton-gin, and the
      rice-cleanser.

Beneath thy look, O Maternal,
With these, and else, and with their own strong hands, the
      Heroes harvest.

All gather, and all harvest;
(Yet but for thee, O Powerful! not a scythe might swing, as
      now, in security;
Not a maize-stalk dangle, as now, its silken tassels in peace.)

13

Under Thee only they harvest—even but a wisp of hay, under
      thy great face, only;
Harvest the wheat of Ohio, Illinois, Wisconsin—every barbed
      spear, under thee;
Harvest the maize of Missouri, Kentucky, Tennessee—each ear
      it its light-green sheath,
Gather the hay to its myriad mows, in the odorous,
      tranquil barns,
Oats to their bins—the white potato, the buckwheat of
      Michigan, to theirs;
Gather the cotton in Mississippi or Alabama—dig and
      hoard the golden, the sweet potato of Georgia
      and the Carolinas,

Clip the wool of California or Pennsylvania,
Cut the flax in the Middle States, or hemp, or tobacco
          in the Borders,
Pick the pea and the bean, or pull apples from the trees, or
          bunches of grapes from the vines,
Or aught that ripens in all These States, or North or South,
Under the beaming sun, and under Thee.

SPARKLES FROM THE WHEEL

First published in 1870

1

WHERE THE CITY'S ceaseless crowd moves on, the live-long day,
Withdrawn, I join a group of children watching–I pause aside
          with them.

By the curb, toward the edge of the flagging,
A knife-grinder works at his wheel, sharpening a great knife;
Bending over, he carefully holds it to the stone–by foot
          and knee,
With measur'd tread, he turns rapidly–As he presses with light
          but firm hand,
Forth issue, then, in copious golden jets,
Sparkles from the wheel.

2

The scene, and all its belongings–how they seize and
          affect me!
The sad, sharp-chinn'd old man, with worn clothes, and broad
          shoulder-band of leather;

Myself, effusing and fluid—a phantom curiously floating—now
       here absorb'd and arrested;

The group, (an unminded point, set in a vast surrounding;)
The attentive, quiet children—the loud, proud, restive base of
       the streets;
The low, hoarse purr of the whirling stone—the
       light-press'd blade,
Diffusing, dropping, sideways-darting, in tiny showers of gold,
Sparkles from the wheel.

As a Strong Bird on Pinions Free

Commencement Poem, Dartmouth College, N.H., June 26, 1872,
on invitation United Literary Societies
First published in "As a Strong Bird," etc., 1872

1

As a strong bird on pinions free,
Joyous the amplest spaces heavenward cleaving,
Such be the thought I'd think to-day of thee, America,
Such be the recitative I'd bring to-day for thee.

The conceits of the poets of other lands I bring thee not,
Nor the compliments that have served their turn so long,
Nor rhyme—nor the classics—nor perfume of foreign court, or
       indoor library;
But on odor I'd bring to-day as from forests of pine in the
       north, in Maine—or breath of an Illinois prairie,
With open airs of Virginia, or Georgia, or Tennessee—or from
       Texas uplands, or Florida's glades,

With presentment of Yellowstone's scenes, or Yosemite;
And murmuring under, pervading all, I'd bring the rustling
        sea-sound,
That endlessly sounds from the two great seas of the world.

And for thy subtler sense, subtler refrains, O Union!
Preludes of intellect tallying these and thee—mind-formulas
        fitted for thee—real, and sane, and large as these
        and thee;
Thou, mounting higher, diving deeper than we knew—thou
        transcendental Union!
By thee Fact to be justified—blended with Thought;
Thought of Man justified—blended with God:
Through thy Idea—lo! the immortal Reality!
Through thy Reality—lo! the immortal Idea!

2

Brain of the New World! what a task is thine!
To formulate the Modern. . . . . Out of the peerless grandeur of
        the modern,
Out of Thyself—comprising Science—to recast Poems,
        Churches, Art,
(Recast—may-be discard them, end them—May-be their work is
        done— who knows?)
By vision, hand, conception, on the background of the mighty
        past, the dead,
To limn, with absolute faith, the mighty living present.

(And yet, thou living, present brain! heir of the dead, the Old
        World brain!
Thou that lay folded, like an unborn babe, within its folds
        so long!

Thou carefully prepared by it so long!—haply thou but
        unfoldest it—only maturest it;
It to eventuate in thee—the essence of the by-gone time
        contain'd in thee;
Its poems, churches, arts, unwitting to themselves, destined
        with reference to thee,
The fruit of all the Old, ripening to-day in thee.)

3

Sail—sail thy best, ship of Democracy!
Of value is thy freight—'tis not the Present only,
The Past is also stored in thee!
Thou holdest not the venture of thyself alone—not of thy
        western continent alone;
Earth's *resumé* entire floats on thy keel, O ship—is steadied by
        thy spars;
With thee Time voyages in trust—the antecedent nations sink
        or swim with thee;
With all their ancient struggles, martyrs, heroes, epics, wars,
        thou bear'st the other continents;
Theirs, theirs as much as thine, the destination-port
        triumphant:
—Steer, steer with good strong hand and wary eye, O
        helmsman—thou carryest great companions,
Venerable, priestly Asia sails this day with thee,
And royal, feudal Europe sails with thee.

4

Beautiful World of new, superber Birth, that rises to my eyes,
Like a limitless golden cloud, filling the western sky;
Emblem of general Maternity, lifted above all

Sacred shape of the bearer of daughters and sons;
Out of thy teeming womb, thy giant babes in ceaseless
     procession issuing,
Acceding from such gestation, taking and giving continual
     strength and life;
World of the Real! world of the twain in one!
World of the Soul–born by the world of the real alone–led to
     identity, body, by it alone;
Yet in beginning only–incalculable masses of composite,
     precious materials,
By history's cycles forwarded–by every nation, language,
     hither sent,
Ready, collected here–a freer, vast, electric World, to be
     constructed here,
(The true New World–the world of orbic Science, Morals,
     Literatures to come,)
Thou Wonder World, yet undefined, unform'd–neither do I
     define thee;
How can I pierce the impenetrable blank of the future?
I feel thy ominous greatness, evil as well as good;
I watch thee, advancing, absorbing the present, transcending
     the past;
I see thy light lighting and thy shadow shadowing, as if the
     entire globe;
But I do not undertake to define thee–hardly to
     comprehend thee;
I but thee name–thee prophecy–as now!
I merely thee ejaculate!

Thee in thy future;
Thee in thy only permanent life, career–thy own unloosen'd
     mind–thy soaring spirit;

Thee as another equally needed sun, America – radiant, ablaze,
     swift-moving, fructifying all;
Thee! risen in thy potent cheerfulness and joy – thy endless,
     great hilarity!
(Scattering for good the cloud that hung so long – that weigh'd
     so long upon the mind of man,
The doubt, suspicion, dread, of gradual, certain decadence
     of man;)
Thee in thy larger, saner breeds of Female, Male – thee in thy
     athletes, moral, spiritual, South, North, West, East,
(To thy immortal breasts, Mother of All, thy every daughter,
     son, endear'd alike, forever equal;)
Thee in thy own musicians, singers, artists, unborn yet,
     but certain;
Thee in thy moral wealth and civilization (until which thy
     proudest material wealth and civilization must remain
     in vain;)
Thee in thy all-supplying, all-enclosing Worship – thee in no
     single bible, saviour, merely,
Thy saviours countless, latent within thyself – thy bibles
     incessant, within thyself, equal to any, divine as any;
Thee in an education grown of thee – in teachers, studies,
     students, born of thee;
Thee in thy democratic fêtes, en masse – thy high original
     festivals, operas, lecturers, preachers;
Thee in thy ultimata, (the preparations only now completed –
     the edifice on sure foundations tied,)
Thee in thy pinnacles, intellect, thought – thy topmost rational
     joys – thy love, and godlike aspiration,
In thy resplendent coming literati – thy full-lung'd orators – thy
     sacerdotal bards – kosmic savans,
These! these in thee, (certain to come,) to-day I prophecy.

5

Land tolerating all – accepting all – not for the good alone – all
        good for thee;
Land in the realms of God to be a realm unto thyself;
Under the rule of God to be a rule unto thyself.

(Lo! where arise three peerless stars,
To be thy natal stars, my country – Ensemble – Evolution –
        Freedom,
Set in the sky of Law.)

Land of unprecedented faith – God's faith!
Thy soil, thy very subsoil, all upheav'd;
The general inner earth, so long, so sedulously draped over,
        now and hence for what it is, boldly laid bare,
Open'd by thee to heaven's light, for benefit or bale.

Not for success alone;
Not to fair-sail unintermitted always;
The storm shall dash thy face – the murk of war, and worse
        than war, shall cover thee all over;
(Wert capable of war – its tug and trials? Be capable of peace,
        its trials;
For the tug and mortal stain of nations come at last in
        peace – not war;)
In many a smiling mask death shall approach, beguiling
        thee – thou in disease shalt swelter;
The livid cancer spread its hideous claws, clinging upon thy
        breasts, seeking to strike thee deep within;
Consumption of the worst – moral consumption – shall rouge
        thy face with hectic:

But thou shalt face thy fortunes, thy diseases, and surmount
      them all,
Whatever they are to-day, and whatever through time they
      may be,
They each and all shall lift, and pass away, and cease
      from thee;
While thou, Time's spirals rounding—out of thyself, thyself still
      extricating, fusing,
Equable, natural, mystical Union thou—(the mortal with
      immortal blent,)
Shalt soar toward the fulfilment of the future—the spirit of the
      body and the mind,
The Soul—its destinies.

The Soul, its destinies—the real real,
(Purport of all these apparitions of the real;)
In thee, America, the Soul, its destinies;
Thou globe of globes! thou wonder nebulous!
By many a throe of heat and cold convuls'd—(by these
      thyself solidifying;)
Thou mental, moral orb! thou New, indeed new, Spiritual
      World!
The Present holds thee not—for such vast growth as thine—for
      such unparallel'd flight as thine,
The Future only holds thee, and can hold thee.

. . .

ESSAYS

Observations on Walt Whitman

BY

T. S. ELIOT

I DO NOT mean to suggest that all discontent is divine, or that all self-righteousness is loathesome. On the contrary, both Tennyson and Whitman made satisfaction almost magnificent. It is not the best aspect of their verse; if neither of them had more, neither of them would be still a great poet. But Whitman succeeds in making America as it was, just as Tennyson made England as it was, into something grand and significant. You cannot quite say that either was deceived, and you cannot at all say that either was insincere, or the victim of popular cant. They had the faculty—Whitman perhaps more prodigiously than Tennyson—of transmuting the real into an ideal. Whitman had the ordinary desires of the flesh; for him there was no chasm between the real and the ideal, such as opened before the horrified eyes of Baudelaire. But this, and the "frankness" about sex for which he is either extolled or mildly reproved did not spring from any particular honesty or clearness of vision: it sprang from what may be called either "idealisation" or a faculty for make-believe, according as we are disposed. There is, fundamentally, no difference between the Whitman frankness and the Tennyson delicacy, except in its relation to public opinion of the time. And Tennyson liked monarchs, and Whitman liked presidents. Both were conservative, rather than reactionary or revolutionary; that is to say, they believed explicitly in progress, and believed implicitly that progress consists in things remaining much as they are.

If this were all there is to Whitman, it would still be a great deal; he would remain a great representative of America, but emphatically of an America which no longer exists. It is not the America of Mr. Scott Fitzgerald, or Mr. Dos Passos, or Mr. Hemingway – to name some of the more interesting of contemporary American writers. If I may draw still one more comparison, it is with Hugo. Beneath all the declamations there is another tone, and behind all the illusions there is another vision. When Whitman speaks of the lilacs or of the mocking-bird, his theories and beliefs drop away like a needless pretext.

T.S. (Thomas Stearns) Eliot (1888–1965) was an American-born expatriate who became a celebrated British citizen. A Nobel Prize-winning poet and a literary critic, he wrote *Prufrock and Other Observations* and *The Wasteland*, as well as seminal works of criticism, including *On Poetry and Poets*.

Whitman

BY

D.H. LAWRENCE

WHITMAN IS THE greatest of the Americans. One of the greatest
poets of the world, in him an element of falsity troubles us
still. Something is wrong; we cannot be quite at ease with
his greatness.

This may be our own fault. But we sincerely feel that
something is overdone in Whitman; there is something that is
too much. Let us get over our quarrel with him first.

All the Americans, when they have trodden new ground,
seem to have been conscious of making a breach in the
established order. They have been self-conscious about it.
They have felt that they were trespassing, transgressing, or
going very far, and this has given a certain stridency, or
portentousness, or luridness to their manner. Perhaps that is
because the steps were taken so rapidly. From Franklin to
Whitman is a hundred years. It might be a thousand.

The Americans have finished in haste, with a certain
violence and violation, that which Europe began two thousand
years ago or more. Rapidly they have returned to lay open the
secrets which the Christian epoch has taken two thousand
years to close up.

With the Greeks started the great passion for the ideal, the
passion for translating all consciousness, into terms of spirit
and ideal or idea. They did this in reaction from the vast old
world which was dying in Egypt. But the Greeks, though they
set out to conquer the animal or sensual being in man, did not
set out to annihilate it. This was left for the Christians.

The Christians, phase by phase, set out actually to
annihilate the sensual being in man. They insisted that man

was in his reality *pure spirit*, and that he was perfectible as such. And this was their business, to achieve such a perfection.

They worked from a profound inward impulse, the Christian religious impulse. But their proceeding was the same, in living extension, as that of he Greek esoterics, such as John the Evangel or Socrates. They proceeded, by will and by exaltation, to overcome *all* the passions and all the appetites and prides.

Now, so far, in Europe, the conquest of the lower self has been objective. That is, man has moved from a great impulse within himself, unconscious. But once the conquest has been effected, there is a temptation for the conscious mind to return and finger and explore, just as tourists now explore battle-fields. This self-conscious *mental* provoking of sensation and reaction in the great affective centres is what we call sentimentalism or sensationalism. The mind returns upon the affective centres, and sets up in them a deliberate reaction.

And this is what all the Americans do, beginning with Crêvecœur, Hawthorne, Poe, all the transcendentalists, Melville, Prescott, Wendell Holmes, Whitman, they are all guilty of this provoking of mental reactions in the physical self, passions exploited by the mind. In Europe, men like Balzac and Dickens, Tolstoi and Hardy, still act direct from the passional motive, and not inversely, from mental provocation. But the æsthetes and symbolists, from Baudelaire and Maeter-linck and Oscar Wilde onwards, and nearly all later Russian, French, and English novelists set up their reactions in the mind and reflect them by a secondary process down into the body. This makes a vicious living and a spurious art. It is one of the last and most fatal effects of idealism. Everything becomes self-conscious and spurious, to the pitch of madness. It is the madness of the world of to-day. Europe and America are all alike; all the nations self-consciously provoking their own passional reactions from the mind, and *nothing* spontaneous.

And this is our accusation against Whitman, as against the others. Too often he deliberately, self-consciously *affects* himself. It puts us off, it makes us dislike him. But since such self-conscious secondariness is a concomitant of all American art, and yet not sufficiently so to prevent that art from being of rare quality, we must get over it. The excuse is that the Americans have had to perform in a century a curve which it will take Europe much longer to finish, if ever she finishes it.

Whitman has gone further, in actual living expression, than any man, it seems to me. Dostoevsky has burrowed underground into the decomposing psyche. But Whitman has gone forward in life-knowledge. It is he who surmounts the grand climacteric of our civilization.

Whitman enters on the last phase of spiritual triumph. He really arrives at that stage of infinity which the seers sought. By subjecting the *deepest centres* of the lower self, he attains the maximum consciousness in the higher self: a degree of extensive consciousness greater, perhaps, than any man in the modern world.

We have seen Dana and Melville, the two adventurers, setting out to conquer the last vast *element*, with the spirit. We have seen Melville touching at last the far end of the immemorial, prehistoric Pacific civilization, in "Typee." We have seen his terrific cruise into universality.

Now we must remember that the way, even towards a state of infinite comprehension, is through the externals towards the quick. And the vast elements, the cosmos, the big things, the universals, these are always the externals. These are met first and conquered first. That is why science is so much easier than art. The quick is the living being, the quick of quicks is the individual soul. And it is here, at the quick, that Whitman proceeds to find the experience of infinitude, his vast extension, or concentrated intensification into Allness. He carries the conquest to its end.

If we read his pæans, his chants of praise and deliverance
and accession, what do we find? All-embracing, indiscrim-
inate, passional acceptance; surges of chaotic vehemence of
invitation and embrace, catalogues, lists, enumerations.
"Whoever you are, to you endless announcements!..."
"And of these one and all I weave the song of myself." "Lovers,
endless lovers."

Continually the one cry: I am everything and everything is
me. I accept everything in my consciousness; nothing is
rejected: –

> I am he that aches with amorous love;
> Does the earth gravitate? does not all matter,
>   aching, attract all matter?
> So the body of me to all I meet or know.

At last everything is conquered. At last the lower centres are
conquered. At last the lowest plane is submitted to the highest.
At last there is nothing more to conquer. At last all is one, all
is love, even hate is love, even flesh is spirit. The great
oneness, the experience of infinity, the triumph of the living
spirit, which at last includes everything, is here accomplished.

It is man's accession into wholeness, his knowledge in full.
Now he is united with everything. Now he embraces every-
thing into himself in a oneness. Whitman is drunk with the
new wine of this new great experience, really drunk with the
strange wine of infinitude. So he pours forth his words, his
chants of praise and acclamation. It is man's maximum state of
consciousness, his highest state of spiritual being. Supreme
spiritual consciousness, and the divine drunkenness of
supreme consciousness. It is reached through embracing love.
"And whoever walks a furlong without sympathy walks to his
own funeral dresst in his shroud." And this supreme state,
once reached, shows us the One Identity in everything,
Whitman's cryptic *One Identity*.

Thus Whitman becomes in his own person the whole world, the whole universe, the whole eternity of time. Nothing is rejected. Because nothing opposes him. All adds up to one in him. Item by item he identifies himself with the universe, and this accumulative identity he calls Democracy, En Masse, One Identity, and so on.

But this is the last and final truth, the last truth is at the quick. And the quick is the single individual soul, which is never more than itself, though it embrace eternity and infinity, and never *other* than itself, though it include all men. Each vivid soul is unique, and though one soul embrace another, and include it, still it cannot *become* that other soul, or lovingly disposess that other soul. In extending himself, Whitman still remains himself; he does not become the other man, or the other woman, or the tree, or the universe: in spite of Plato.

Which is the maximum truth, though it appears so small in contrast to all these infinites, and En Masses, and Democracies, and Almightynesses. The essential truth is that a man is himself, and only himself, throughout all his greatnesses and extensions and intensifications.

The second truth which we must bring as a charge against Whitman is the one we brought before, namely, that his Allness, his One Identity, his En Masse, his Democracy, is only a half-truth—an enormous half-truth. The other half is Jehovah, and Egypt, and Sennacherib: the other form of Allness, terrible and grand, even as in the Psalms.

Now Whitman's way to Allness, he tells us, is through endless sympathy, merging. But in merging you must merge away from something, as well as towards something, and in sympathy you must depart from one point to arrive at another. Whitman lays down this law of sympathy as the one law, the direction of merging as the one direction. Which is obviously wrong. Why not a right-about-turn? Why not turn slip back to the point from which you started to merge? Why not *that* direction, the reverse of merging, back to the single and overweening self? Why not, instead of endless dilation of sympathy, the retraction into isolation and pride?

Why not? The heart and its systole diastole, the shuttle comes and goes, even the sun rises and sets. We know, as a matter of fact, that all life lies between two poles. The direction is two-fold. Whitman's *one direction* becomes a hideous tyranny once he has attained his goal of Allness. His One Identity is a prison of horror, once realized. For identities are manifold and each jewel-like, different as a sapphire from an opal. And the motion of merging becomes at last a vice, a nasty degeneration, as when tissue breaks down into a mucous slime. There must be the sharp retraction from isolation, following the expansion into unification, otherwise the integral being is overstrained and will break, break down like disintegrating issue into slime, imbecility, epilepsy, vice, like Dostoevsky.

And one word more. Even if you reach the state of infinity, you can't sit down there. You just physically can't. You either have to strain still further into universality and become vaporish, or slimy: or you have to hold your toes and sit tight and practise Nirvana; or you have to come back to common dimensions, each your pudding and blow your nose and be just yourself; or die and have done with it. A grand experience is a grand experience. It brings a man to his maximum. But even at his maximum a man is not more than himself. When he is infinite he is still himself. He still has a nose to wipe. The state of infinity is *only* a state, even if it be the supreme one.

But in achieving this state Whitman opened a new field of living. He drives on to the very centre of life and sublimates even this into consciousness. Melville hunts the remote white whale of the deepest passional body, tracks it down. But it is

Whitman who captures the whale. The pure sensual body of
man, at its deepest remoteness and intensity, this is the White
Whale. And this is what Whitman captures.

He seeks his consummation through one continual ecstacy:
the ecstacy of *giving himself*, and of being taken. The ecstacy of
his own reaping and merging with another, with others; the
sword-cut of sensual death. Whitman's motion is always the
motion of *giving himself*: This is my body–take, and eat. It is
the great sacrament. He knows nothing of the other sacrament,
the sacrament in pride, where the communicant envelops the
victim and host in a flame of ecstatic consuming, sensual
gratification, and triumph.

But he is concerned with others beside himself: with
woman, for example. But what is woman to Whitman? Not
much? She is a great function–no more. Whitman's "athletic
mothers of these States" are depressing. Muscles and wombs:
functional creatures–no more.

> As I see my soul reflected in Nature.
> As I see through a mist, One with inexpressible
>   completeness, sanity, beauty,
> See the bent head and arms folded over the
>   breast, the Female I see.

That is all. The woman is reduced, really, to a submissive
function. She is no longer an individual being with a living
soul. She must fold her arms and bend her head and submit to
her functioning capacity. Function of sex, function of birth.

> This is the nucleus–after the child is born of
>   woman, man is born of woman,
> This the bath of birth, this the merge of small
>   and large, and the outlet again–

Acting from the last and profoundest centres, man acts
womanless. It is no longer a question of race continuance. It is

a question of sheer, ultimate being, the perfection of life, nearest to death. Acting from these centres, man is an extreme being, the unthinkable warrior, creator, mover, and maker.

And the polarity is between man and man. Whitman alone of all moderns has known this positively. Others have known it negatively, *pour épater les bourgeois*. But Whitman knew it positively, in its tremendous knowledge, knew the extremity, the perfectness, and the fatality.

Even Whitman becomes grave, tremulous, before the last dynamic truth of life. In *Calamus* he does not shout. He hesitates: he is reluctant, wistful. But none the less he goes on. And he tells the mystery of manly love, the love of comrades. Continually he tells us the same truth: the new world will be built upon the love of comrades, the new great dynamic of life will be manly love. Out of this inspiration the creation of the future.

The strange Calamus has its pink-tinged root by the pond, and it sends up its leaves of comradeship, comrades at one root, without the intervention of woman, the female. This comradeship is to be the final cohering principle of the new world, the new Democracy. It is the cohering principle of perfect soldiery, as he tells in "Drum Taps." It is the cohering principle of final *unison* in creative activity. And it is extreme and alone, touching the confines of death. It is something terrible to bear, terrible to be responsible for. It is the soul's last and most vivid responsibility, the responsibility for the circuit of final friendship, comradeship, manly love.

> Yet you are beautiful to me you faint-tinged roots,
> you make me think of death,
> Death is beautiful from you, (what indeed is finally
> beautiful except death and love?)
> O I think it is not for life I am chanting here my
> chant of lovers, I think it must be for death.

> For how calm, how solemn it grows to ascend to the
> atmosphere of lovers,
> Death or life I am then indifferent, my soul declines
> to prefer,
> (I am not sure but the high soul of lovers welcomes
> death most,)
> Indeed O death, I think now these leaves mean
> precisely the same as you mean —

Here we have the deepest, finest Whitman, the Whitman who knows the extremity of life, and of the soul's responsibility. He has come near now to death, in his creative life. But creative life must come near to death, to link up the mystic circuit. The pure warriors must stand on the brink of death. So must the men of a pure creative nation. We shall have no beauty, no dignity, no essential freedom otherwise. And so it is from Sea-Drift, where the male bird sings the lost female: not that she is lost, but lost to him who has had to go beyond her, to sing on the edge of the great sea, in the night. It is the last voice on the shore.

> Whereto answering, the sea,
> Delaying not, hurrying not,
> Whisper'd to me through the night, and very plainly
> before daybreak,
> Lisp'd to me the low and delicious word death,
> And again death, death, death, death,
> Hissing melodious, neither like the bird not like my
> arous'd child's heart,
> But edging near as privately for me rustling at
> my feet,
> Creeping thence steadily up to my ears and laving
> me softly all over,
> Death, death, death, death, death —

What a great poet Whitman is: great like a great Greek. For him the last enclosures have fallen, he finds himself on the shore of the last sea. The extreme of life: so near to death. It is a hushed, deep responsibility. And what is the responsibility? It is for the new great era of mankind. And upon what is this new era established? On the perfect circuits of vital flow between human beings. First, the great sexless normal relation between individuals, simple sexless friendships, unison of family, and clan, and nation, and group. Next, the powerful sex relation between man and woman, culminating in the eternal orbit of marriage. And, finally, the sheer friendship, the love between comrades, the manly love which alone can create a new era of life.

The one state, however, does not annul the other: it fulfils the other. Marriage is the great step beyond friendship, and family, and nationality, but it does not supersede these. Marriage should only give repose and perfection to the great previous bonds and relationships. A wife or husband who sets about to annul the old, pre-marriage affections and connections ruins the foundations of marriage. And so with the last, extremest love, the love of comrades. The ultimate comradeship which sets about to destroy marriage destroys its own *raison d'être*. The ultimate comradeship is the final progression from marriage; it is the last seedless flower of pure beauty, beyond purpose. But if it destroys marriage it makes itself purely deathly. In its beauty, the ultimate comradeship flowers on the brink of death. But it flowers from the root of all life upon the blossoming tree of life.

The life-circuit now depends entirely upon the sex-unison of marriage. This circuit must never be broken. But it must be still surpassed. We cannot help the laws of life.

If marriage is sacred, the ultimate comradeship is utterly sacred, since it has no ulterior motive whatever, like procreation. If marriage is eternal, the great bond of life, how much more is this bond eternal, being the great life-circuit which borders on death in all its round. The new, extreme, the sacred relationship of comrades awaits us, and the future of mankind depends on the way in which this relation is entered upon by us. It is a relation between fearless, honorable, self-responsible men, a balance in perfect polarity.

The last phase is entered upon, shakily, by Whitman. It will take us an epoch to establish the new, perfect circuit of our being. It will take an epoch to establish the love of comrades, as marriage is really established now. For fear of going on, forwards, we turn round and destroy, or try to destroy, what lies behind. We are trying to destroy marriage, because we have not the courage to go forward from marriage to the new issue. Marriage must never be wantonly attacked. *True* marriage is eternal; in it we have our consummation and being. But the final consummation lies in that which is beyond marriage.

And when the bond, or circuit of perfect comrades is established, what then, when we are on the brink of death, fulfilled in the vastness of life? Then, at last, we shall know a starry maturity.

Whitman put us on the track years ago. Why has no one gone on from him? The great poet, why does no one accept his greatest word? The Americans are not worthy of their Whitman. They take him like a cocktail, for fun. Miracle that they have not annihilated every word of him. But these miracles happen.

The greatest modern poem! Whitman, at his best, is purely himself. His verse springs sheer from the spontaneous sources of his being. Hence its lovely, lovely form and rhythm: at the best. It is sheer, perfect, *human* spontaneity, spontaneous as a nightingale throbbing, but still controlled, the highest loveliness of human spontaneity, undecorated, unclothed. The whole being is there, sensually throbbing, spiritually quivering, mentally, ideally speaking. It is not, like Swinburne, an exaggeration of the one part of being. It is perfect and whole. The whole soul speaks at once, and is too pure for mechanical assistance of rhyme and measure. The perfect utterance of a concentrated, spontaneous soul. The unforgettable loveliness of Whitman's lines:

> Out of the cradle endlessly rocking.
> *Ave America!*

D.H. (David Herbert) Lawrence (1885–1930) was an English novelist, playwright, and literary critic. While he is best known for his novels, including *Sons and Lovers* and *Women in Love*, he also wrote an insightful anthology of literary criticism, entitled *Studies in Classic American Literature*, from which this essay is excerpted.